FOOTBALLERS'
WIVES

RE

N.N.

FOOTBALLERS' WIVES
Tell Their Tales

Shelley Webb

YELLOW JERSEY PRESS
LONDON

Published by Yellow Jersey Press 1998

2 4 6 8 10 9 7 5 3 1

First published in Great Britain in 1998 by
Yellow Jersey Press
Random House, 20 Vauxhall Bridge Road, London SW1V 2SA

Random House Australia (Pty) Limited
20 Alfred Street, Milsons Point, Sydney,
New South Wales 2061, Australia

Random House New Zealand Limited
18 Poland Road, Glenfield,
Auckland 10, New Zealand

Random House South Africa (Pty) Limited
Endulini, 5A Jubilee Road, Parktown 2193, South Africa

Random House UK Limited Reg. No. 954009

A CIP catalogue record for this book
is available from the British Library

ISBN 0 224 05065 6

Papers used by Random House UK Limited are natural,
recyclable products made from wood grown in sustainable forests.
The manufacturing processes conform to the environmental
regulations of the country of origin

Printed and bound in Great Britain by
Mackays of Chatham PLC

To my parents,
Tony and Coral – whose love and encouragement
have enriched my life immeasurably

and

in memory of Heather Sanchez, 1959–1998

Contents

Foreword   ix
Acknowledgements   xi

Shelley Webb   1
Denise Gallagher   51
Helen Saunders   59
Viv Neate   71
Kirsty Dailly   77
Audrey Bowen   87
Kelly Woan   95
Heather Sanchez   107
Cheryl Hirst   121
Kirstine Fry   129
Brigitte Arscott   137
Lorraine Sass   143
Suzi Walker   155
Karen Wigley   165
Suzy Barnes   177

Foreword

It was 5 a.m. and there was Jimmy McGovern, one of our foremost dramatists, admitting that never in a million years did he expect a football wife to be on the writing course on which he was still holding court after his guest lecture the evening before.

Well, who could blame him. After all, our particular species has been well and truly pigeon-holed into the 'dim bird' category. What's more, we're Malibu-drinking bimbos who live in tacky houses and in the TV drama *The Manageress* even indulged in a three-in-a-bed session with the manager . . .

It was obviously time to begin a pilgrimage to football-wife enlightenment – a journey on which I was joined by 14 fascinating and diverse women, who, with an overwhelming generosity of spirit, entertained and educated me with their own footballing tales.

Over the course of the year when I travelled the country to meet these inspirational women my own personal crisis was at its height. Listening to the stories which so often mirrored my own, and hearing how they coped with the madness that so often is the football world, went no small way towards aiding my healing process. For that alone I owe all my footballing wives my eternal thanks.

Acknowledgements

I was once listening to a playwright talk about his work. Did you enjoy writing the play? he was asked. Only when it was finished, came the reply. I now know exactly what he meant and to all those people whose enthusiasm, encouragement and suggestions sustained me along the way – a very big thank-you.

Particular thanks go to David Downs, the Reading FC historian; Amelia Clark at Derby County; Rory Mulvihill, at Spencer, Ewin and Mulvihill; and Sally Coxon, Jon Holmes, Diana van Bunnens and Geoff Wightman at Park Associates.

Neil, I don't know how you and Luke and Josh put up with living with the mountains of mess over so many months. Much love.

Finally my greatest thanks must go to my editor Rachel Cugnoni. It was her vision and faith in me that brought me to this project and her commitment and optimism which sustained me through the rocky times. How we ever got through it without you reading me the Riot Act, Rachel, I'll never know. But many, many thanks. I couldn't have done it without you.

FOOTBALLERS' WIVES

Shelley Webb

Shelley Webb is a writer and broadcaster. She is married to former England international Neil, who began his career at Reading FC and went on to play for Portsmouth, Nottingham Forest and Manchester United.

A Tommy Lawton thunderbolt. The Elm Park crowd held their breath as the ball just shaved the post only to pole-axe a youngster sitting on the wall beside the goal. The 13-year-old lad was carried out and the Reading crowd trembled at the thought of what the great Lawton, newly signed for Notts County, would do in the match proper – for the unlucky boy had been KO-ed in the warm-up. That young fan was my father; the same boy who grew up to play against an ageing Lawton; the same lad who used to cycle from Reading up to Stamford Bridge to watch Chelsea, ensuring that blue was the colour of my fan's heart; the same dad who suggested I go and watch a Reading reserve match to get over being chucked by the head boy, the same man who unselfconsciously bowed when I introduced him to the late great Sir Matt Busby, the same father who once introduced me as Neil Webb's wife – I kicked him.

Growing up with such a hero for a father I couldn't help but fall in love with our national game. Inevitable then, you might think, that I fell for a footballer and exchanged the football daughter tag for the one of wife. Actually it could easily have been very different. My mother had been a Silhouette, one of the dancing troupe of lovelies who adorned such gems from the era of BBC television variety as *The Billy Cotton Band Show*. She was also Cliff Richard's 'Walkin', Talkin', Livin' Doll' when he sang the hit first time around, and when she wasn't doing live telly was entertaining, among others, Winston Churchill at the Savoy. But as fate would have it my sister got the long, slim, ballerina pins. I lumbered through

3

adolescence on my father's short, fat and occasionally hairy midfield legs – the rough with the smooth, you might say. My destiny was sealed.

Not that I really had any grand scheme that the white knight riding towards my goal should be sporting shin-pad armour and a jockstrap codpiece. Indeed, nothing could be further from the truth – I positively looked down my nose at anyone consorting with a footballer, because of course the species had gone markedly down-hill since my father's day. But when the head boy gives you the elbow after a year of furtive fumbling behind the lockers between history and geography – well it can do strange things to a 17-year-old girl.

Westwood School – For Slappers – as some unkind soul had graffitied on to the entrance sign – was sepa-rated from Reading Football Club by Prospect Park, and prospecting a-plenty went on in the woods which con-veniently bisected the park – a great deal of it between Reading's apprentice footballers and young Westwood women of a generous disposition.

'I'll never go out with a footballer,' I used to declare as yet another Westwood girl stumbled out of the woods on her wedges. My classmates would nod sagely but we all secretly yearned to know what it was exactly that made these particular young women so in demand. But stoop to be a football groupie to find out? Never.

My father meanwhile had exchanged life as a player to manage local sides in the Reading area. He had also become a vice-president at Reading FC so when the big heave-ho came from the head boy – on the phone from Belfast – a Reading reserve match seemed to offer certain cathartic possibilities. Possibilities that appeared all the more attractive when I realised that the opposition was the mighty Spurs and that the wunderkind Glenn Hoddle was playing. This doyen of footballing skill and good conduct wouldn't have chucked his girlfriend on the phone, mumbling about Guinness and wild oats . . .

So I was at a footy match with my dad and Glenn was on the park – who needed a boyfriend? Then just when I was marvelling at the fourth Tottenham goal something hit me out of the Elm Park night sky. I think they call it love at first sight. 'Who's the Reading sweeper, the one that walks like a monkey?' 'Webb,' replied my dad helpfully. 'Bit of a prospect.' As in going to go far, rather than one of the park brigade, I hoped. But I didn't get the chance to find out. Oh yes he did come into the tea-room afterwards and our eyes met and lingered and then, well, nothing. Perhaps he had a girlfriend? No, my dad discovered on the grapevine. Then I obviously wasn't his type . . . but apparently he'd been asking about me. So, ever the optimist I kept the Reading reserve attendance figures buoyant and regularly we smiled a greeting across a cuppa but the guy with the gorgeous legs – OK, I admit it – was as shy as me. It didn't help that his mate and fellow apprentice, who obviously came from the same gene pool as the head boy, told him he couldn't possibly fancy me because I had gappy teeth.

So there I was rapidly losing any credibility as a Chelsea fan when Cupid intervened and led to an unlikely meeting in the Boar's Head, early one Saturday evening. We were on a girls' night out when I suddenly spotted him. What was this demi-god, supposedly a worshipper at the shrine of athleticism and good health, doing in this dive? Hail the intermediary in the form of my friend Suzanne who discovered that their reserve match had been cancelled en route. Indeed, sick to death of my sighing and mooning, she seized the initiative. 'Do you fancy my mate?' 'She's all right.' 'D'you want to go out with her?' 'OK.' Suzanne, you idiot, what are you doing? I squirmed from the other side of the bar when what I really meant is you wonderful, brilliant mate. And so it was fixed – the roller disco the next evening at Top Rank. A date – and neither of us had uttered a word.

But of course he wouldn't turn up, or so I thought as I nervously clocked the queue outside the disco and I'd literally spent all afternoon getting ready, pacing the house watching the minutes tick by – even *The Big Match* couldn't take away the butterflies in my stomach. Later I realised this was a strange foretaste of the pre-match nerves I would come to suffer before any of Neil's games. I thought about trying to sell my ticket and then I saw him. Right at the front of the line. He must have got here before *The Big Match* – what a sacrifice. And the rest, as they say, is history.

Well, not quite. Suzanne, the best friend a girl could ever have, arrived and we discovered as we escorted him around the rink that this shy, gentle guy was really rubbish at roller-skating. No matter, because it gave me plenty of time in the darkened corners of the disco to discover his strengths. And believe you me it wasn't his salary. I was earning more working on a Saturday at Boots than he was as an apprentice when he took home the princely sum of £14 per week. Then at 9.30 p.m. he said he'd have to go. I couldn't believe it and implored him to ask his dad for a little extra time, secretly fearing that I'd never see him again. The phone call did not go well. He was red-carded and I was banned from his life. However, refs were more lenient in those days and on receipt of my solemn declaration that I would not come between Neil and his football the romance continued. As for my A levels . . . well, you try analysing the domino effect in South-East Asia when you're a teenager in love.

So Neil became a regular first-team player for Reading, scored the odd goal or two and flirted with the promise many people saw in him. At 19 we got engaged but then football – or rather its fringe benefits – led to a break-up as Neil succumbed to the charms of Portsmouth Football Club's groupies.

Of course there were young women who hung around Elm Park but they were just another version of the Westwood School variety. On the odd occasion when I gave *King Lear* or Chiang Kai-shek a miss and picked Neil up after training, the female coterie hanging around the ground were a motley group. Except for one who had the most amazing yellow tresses – a real-life Rapunzel with the added advantage of an ample bosom to help haul in her footballer. But even when this group got themselves match-day jobs behind the Wagon Wheel and Bovril counters – employment which strangely necessitated a second-half parade along the touchline – I gazed down on them with smug satisfaction from my seat in the stand alongside the other Reading wives and girlfriends.

So when Neil was transferred to Portsmouth, another third division team, I complacently felt that my engage-ment ring and fledgling journalistic career – cub reporter on the *Reading Evening Post* – were weighty bulwarks against the tide of the good-time groupies, even though I'd decided to carry on living and working in Reading. But I just hadn't bargained for the Bunker Girls – bronzed, blonde and bristling for action. Indeed, the females flocking to the Pompey players' favourite wine bar were the Hydra of Hampshire: see off one who had been pawing at your man and another would be playing footsie or following him to the Gents. Talk about intimi-dation. One of these sirens only had to flash a smile in our direction and I was instantly crushed. The whole of Pompey seemed to be swathed in a sea of long, tanned limbs while I could feel my midfielder's legs balloon and blotch as rumours of the regular requisitioning of the wine bar's rooftop for extra training initiatives curdled what was left of my stick-on smile. So I stopped going to the Bunker. But you couldn't keep me away from the football.

It was a crazy spring in Portsmouth that season of 82–83. The club was heading for promotion and the town was on a roll. My first visit to Portsmouth's ground, Fratton Park, was when Neil was still with Reading. The Berkshire club were then averaging 3,000 fans at home. But there must have been four times that many supporters at this grand old stadium in Portsmouth – filled to the rafters and reverberating with the Pompey chimes. 'Play up Pompey. Pompey play up.' It was intoxicating – this was a southern footballing town with a passion for the game as intense as any up north.

Such was the clamour of away support that British Rail would lay on the 'Pompey Special' and I'd join several hundred hardy souls at some ungodly hour to catch a train up to one or other of the far-flung corners of the third division football map. I say hardy, but some of them were just plain hard – fans whose idea of supporting their team involved acting out the *Mad Max* trilogy in its entirety. When I paid my money and travelled half the length of the country I wanted to *see* a game of football but the return journey was usually taken up by explaining to these 'fans' exactly how Pompey scored their goals. You see, they'd been mightily occupied before the match indulging in a little exchange mechanism with the opposing fans involving bottles and maybe the odd brick too. And rather than make it inside in time for kick-off, they had been left to rest temporarily at Her Majesty's pleasure in the meat wagons that adorned the streets.

Maybe it's a boy/girl thing. A platform guard at a Midlands railway station certainly thought so. We'd pulled in en route to Blackburn, I think it was, and I was huddled in a corner, turning over the pages of a book with my nose – the heating having broken down it was far too cold to risk a hand out of a sleeve – when there was a tap at the window. It was the platform guard frantically gesturing and looking highly concerned. 'Quick, Miss. You're on the wrong train. This is a football special.' It took me some time to convince him that there was not some gang of Pompey pirates holding me against my will. You see, women have always gone to football but it was still unusual to see one travelling alone. But was I ever scared? Well, I usually sat down and the stands were largely immune to trouble, although I remember seats flying around my head one Pompey away game but I still wasn't frightened. Of course we were always frog-marched into Millwall's Old Den but that was to be expected since there had always been bad blood between Pompey and the east London side. Also I never wore colours – but that wasn't because I was fearful it would mark me out, but because of the schizophrenic nature of being a football wife whose football heart belonged to another. So although I diligently followed and indeed came to care for the club which was at the time paying our mortgage, I'd always have a radio clasped furtively to my ear to find out how my boys in blue were doing.

But there was one trip to Doncaster that I remember with unease and a retrospective sense of foreboding. It was to be my first taste of law and order policing, South Yorkshire style. With promotion to the old second division very much on the cards a large contingent of Pompey supporters arrived by train. But the welcome from the police was anything but warm as we were hustled on to buses and then dropped off on a deserted patch of land some way from the stadium. Of course this close attention by the police on foot and horseback was something that we experienced on most away trips but as we were harried and harangued there was a distinctly ugly tone to the control measures. And indeed on our jubilant return to the railway station – Pompey had won and Neil had scored – we were kept for what seemed like hours in a tunnel under the station to wait for the train. Close proximity to your fellow fan has always been a part of football culture – a synthesis of soul and support directed as one towards the lads. But after a while even the Pompey chimes ceased as we sweated uncomfortably in the gloom. At last the police bar lifted and we moved shouting and singing towards the train and home. On reflection I don't think I was frightened, just uncomfortable. But why had they kept us down in the tunnel so long when we could have waited on the platform? It was quite simple, really. We were all being treated as potential hooligans and therefore didn't warrant the respect an ordinary citizen has of right. It was this fatal flaw at the root of the Thatcherite law and order policing that was to have such tragic consequences when I went to a match at Hillsborough just six years later.

But Hillsborough was the venue for an FA Cup semi-final match, a million miles away from winning the third division championship. Or was it? – because the city of Portsmouth was delirious with happiness as their team not only gained promotion but won the third division title too. The club organised an open-topped bus to take the players and their families and of course the trophy through the city to a Guildhall reception. There were literally thousands of people in the square and they all cheered and waved and sang as the trophy was held aloft from the Guildhall balcony. This was the first of many occasions when I wished I was not up with the dignitaries but celebrating as a fan, among the supporters where the awesome strength of collective passion induces an amazing natural high. Once, during one of my

English degree seminars, we were reading Wordsworth's 'Tintern Abbey' which, our tutor explained, was inspired by the tremendous upsurge of emotion William felt as he strolled through the countryside – an epiphany. Football fans everywhere will know exactly how he felt. It doesn't happen very often but when it does – wow. As this was pre-Pavarotti and *Fever Pitch* though, such a contribution to the discussion was met with withering disdain. But now the literati have become the soccerati and such sentiments have become the stuff of countless articles as writers realise that no longer are you treated like a social degenerate if you admit to a love of football – as well as the fact that since Gazza cried at Italia 90 all things football have pound signs attached.

But what happened in Portsmouth that day was nothing to do with money or high art. It was the consummation of a love affair. A love affair with huge highs and desperate lows, but one that endures. This bonding over many months with supporters from all four of the clubs where Neil spent his league career has meant I still look out for and hope for better things for those teams. At Portsmouth they made him their Player of the Year in the 84–85 season, the only time he ever won such an award. The Pompey fans have had more than their fair share of ups and downs in recent years. But you couldn't have got better than that evening of our third division championship celebration. And of course our celebrations involved the Bunker Girls – more lovely, more luscious and most definitely more lascivious than before.

How the team partied: and nobody noticed, not even Neil, when I left early. He was 19, liked to model himself on George Michael and was a Pompey hero. He had the city and its women on their knees. No wonder it all went to his head. I had been his first real girlfriend. The first to show him there was more to life than football. Now he wanted the world. My phone call the following day was relatively painless. He didn't say much – I didn't eat for three weeks. But there was still the matter of the engagement presents. So for one last time I drove down from Reading to Portsmouth in my old Mini – the one with the engine that cut out when it rained. But the sun shone as I bagged the best presents and successfully negotiated a large cheque in lieu of the tumble-dryer and curtains I'd provided for *chez* Webb. I had to keep my eyes on his pockets to stop the tears. He may have been a big-headed bastard but he was a good-looking one.

As soon as I got back to Reading I booked a holiday to Kos with my mum and dad with the said cheque and, as I was never going out again, got my teeth done. Ever conscious of the gappy-teeth remark from the Reading apprentice, I sank into the dentist's chair and emerged with a metal stud glued to each tooth and thick, shiny wire circumnavigating the inside of my mouth. Jaws had nothing on me. Or on my editor who, fearful I would indeed scare off potential interviewees, banished me to the subs desk. So there I was some six weeks after the break-up, pondering some fruity little headline when my chief sub thrust the phone under my nose. 'It's that bastard on the phone for you.'

'Hello,' I said coolly – well, as coolly as the metal forest in my mouth would allow. Neil's words came out in a torrent. He'd had his ear pierced. He was in Reading, looking after his mum's house. He still had some of my engagement towels. Could I come and get them? Tonight? OK. I put the phone down. How did I feel? An earring – that George Michael thing was getting beyond a joke. His dad would kill him. So he's in Reading. With his South Coast totty in tow, I wondered? Not that I cared. As far as I was concerned I'd had a lucky escape. The only emotional rollercoaster I wanted from football now was from supporting Chelsea. Anyway I was off out with my sister and I was meeting someone. So of course because I had a date I dressed to kill. Shorts that six weeks before I couldn't get over my knees, and a little crop top – no bra. Legs and a mouthful of metal – I don't know which Neil took in first as he opened the door. I told him I couldn't stay long, as my date was waiting. 'You're going out dressed like that,' he mumbled, disappearing through the french windows to punch the outside wall. That's sex, drugs, rock 'n' roll and football, I thought, getting up to go. But somehow I never did make that date. We were married two years later – four days after he signed for Nottingham Forest.

Back then the first division, with the likes of Anfield, Old Trafford, Highbury and the City Ground, could have been on another planet. In the 84–85 season Portsmouth just missed out on joining these luminaries on goal difference to Manchester City. And Neil, in a new role as centre forward, had scored a good few of the Pompey strikes. This hadn't escaped the notice of several first division sides and Graham Turner, then manager of Aston Villa, after agreeing a fee of £250,000 with Portsmouth, invited us up to Birmingham. He struck me as an enthusiastic and honest man, going out of his way to take us round the residential areas and in fact did an excellent job of selling us the club, but then over lunch we met the chairman. Doug Ellis, as one would expect, held court over our repast, pontificating on this and that and things were going quite smoothly for a while. Then for some reason the conversation turned to education as the chairman eulogised over his son's impressive A-level results. Neil then started to recall I had done the same subjects. My kick on his shin was too late and I humiliatingly had to reveal my abysmal grades. But before I had the chance to plead the mitigating circumstances of –

well, I would have thought of something – I was being slapped down with: 'Of course you wouldn't get to university with those grades.' 'No,' I replied meekly but inside I was thinking no, that's right because you're going to pay my husband pots of money so I can be a kept woman and I'll never need to go to poxy university. The silence that followed was embarrassing. Neil squirmed and I gulped down the Villa Chablis. Four years later when I was awarded a first-class honours degree in History and English for one delicious moment I thought I would go and stuff it up Doug Ellis but no, because if there is one thing I have learned about football it's that the only way to stay sane is never to look back. Which we didn't in Birmingham that day. Out future was to lie in the East Midlands with Nottingham Forest.

'Excuse me, young man,' Brian Clough moved to the phone on his desk. 'My shoes need a clean.' An apprentice was duly summoned and took away the offending footwear. 'Now, where were we?' asked the Nottingham Forest manager, padding around in his socks. Well, where we were was, bizarrely, at the point of Clough trying to get Neil to sign a blank contract. Totally bemused, Neil and I couldn't look at each other as we were both possessed with a mixture of mirth and terror. Brian Clough – a name to send a shiver through the boldest of men. Now I was beginning to understand why. You have to remember that this was in the days before agents were commonplace. So with no middleman to advise us, we'd fled from the humiliations at Villa and now it seemed we were diving into the lion's den at Forest. The blank contract had been proffered to Neil after he'd been on a tour of the City Ground. I'd been left on my own in Clough's office. Indeed when I'd tried to contribute to the initial contract talks I was given short shrift: 'I wasn't talking to you, little Miss Busy.' Well, that put me in my place. But when Neil picked up the pen, hypnotised it seemed by Clough's entreaties of trust, I just had to say something. Actually what came out resembled more the noise a small animal might make. Clough considered me, looked away and then asked if I thought I was Sarah Bernhardt – he meant I was trying to usurp his principal actor role in the little drama, didn't he? I wasn't sure, all I know is that as the contract was signed, I was struck dumb. Then I think we had a cup of tea.

In fact Neil's contract was honoured in full and we were both about to embark on what turned out to be the happiest years of our lives, both professionally and personally. As I recall those four years in Nottingham, how I wish we had known that once we left the care of Brian Clough and the City Ground life would never be as carefree again. Dull moments were few and far between with the overwhelming presence of Brian Clough dominating Robin Hood's city. The Yorkshireman was a national institution and his blunt views were eagerly anticipated on the many football shows he graced. But behind the bravado was achievement and commitment of the highest footballing order. For Clough had taken not just one but two mediocre Midlands sides to the League Championship. Derby County and then Forest, who went on to win the European Cup in two consecutive years, have much to thank this enigmatic man for. Clough's record puts him up in the footballing pantheon with the likes of Bill Shankly and Sir Matt Busby and he should have been rewarded with the chance to manage the England team. But those in power shuddered at the thought of having to share the limelight with a man who would challenge and question everything in the pursuit of uncompromising excellence. Interestingly, in the early nineties the England hierarchy, perhaps learning from their mistakes, did give another footballing purist a chance even though his extracurricular activities were thought to be, shall we say, dubious.

And that's exactly what Brian Clough was. A purist. 'Pass it to the nearest red shirt,' was his footballing lexicon. His pre-match talks consisted of an appearance in the dressing room a few minutes before kick-off. There he would examine the ball, tell the players they knew what to do with it and then he was off. Neil told me that on one occasion when the team had trooped back dejectedly to the dressing room at the half-time whistle, 2–0 down, Clough popped his head round the door: 'I'm sorry, lads. I've picked the wrong team,' he said and then disappeared. Of course Forest won that match. His psychological approach to the serious business of football management was legendary and ranged from the Trent training ground runs through the stinging nettles to the ice-lolly treats on the way back to the dressing room. But there were more subtle tests.

In Neil's first season they were playing West Ham at Upton Park. Neil was operating, not entirely happily, on the left side of midfield when Hans Segers, the Forest goalie, injured his knee. These were the days when only one substitute was allowed and on the bench that day was Colin Walsh, a winger. Neil had always fancied himself as a keeper, often going in goal when his school team were far enough in front, and he quickly volunteered to go between the sticks. He put on a fair show and I think only conceded two goals. The next week he was dropped and Clough went public with his belief that Neil had been too eager to get the gloves on, which in the position Forest found themselves, he believed was the easy option. 'Let him show me he can play in midfield before he thinks he can occupy another position,' he told the press. Likewise in a pre-season game against Notts

County, Neil, spotting the goalie off his line, tried to lob him from quite some distance. It didn't come off, but Neil did. And Clough promised he wouldn't hesitate to substitute him again if he ever ignored the easier option of laying the ball off to the nearest red shirt. And then of course there was the discipline on the pitch. You didn't dare fall to the ground unless you basically couldn't walk. Fines came crushing down on your head if you ever argued with the referee, and God help those who took a dive.

Clough demanded good behaviour as well as good football and the team ethos was central to everything. There was no room for prima donnas at the City Ground and oh, how I would have loved to have seen Clough deal with the likes of Tomas Brolin and Emerson. You could argue that there has been a shift in the balance of power towards the players in the last 15 years or so but I don't think Clough would have let that bother him. All it would mean was that Emerson would be stuck in the nettles for as long as it took him to ring his agent on the mobile. He played a slightly more tactical game with the wives, though. On occasion Neil would come home from training and sheepishly explain that the team was popping off to some exotic destination the very next day. Within a few hours the doorbell would ring and flowers, chocolates and magazines would accompany a note of apology from the manager. It was a gesture that didn't stop our grumbling, but the grumbling was a lot more muted as we tucked into the chocolates and arranged the flowers – after all, at least he was acknowledging our existence.

Of course if the truth be told we were all a bit scared of the mighty Clough, particularly with his record for unorthodox action which even the greatest Clough champion had to agree was sometimes a little excessive.

Take this incident early on in the Forest careers of both Neil and Stuart Pearce, newly arrived from Coventry. The players were sipping tea at half-time when Clough came into the dressing room and approached Stuart. 'Stand up,' was the command. The big defender obeyed the Boss and was rewarded with a punch to the stomach. Clough then moved along to a bemused but fortunately prepared Neil to repeat the exercise. Why is still a mystery. But whatever the reasons, Neil adored Brian Clough and Clough was the coach who turned him from a player with potential into one good enough to be chosen to play for England.

Playing a football trivia game with our sons one evening I pulled out the question: 'Who was the 1,000th player to be capped by England?' they were perplexed, and even more so when I told them the player in question was sitting opposite them. They still didn't really believe it even when they studied the answer: Neil Webb. That's how it felt for me the night Neil came on as substitute against West Germany. I had to pinch myself. My husband playing for England – amazing! Pride, honour and intense happiness all mixed into one. But the fixture was in Germany so I had to wait until Turkey at home to see him lining up in an England shirt.

Walking up Wembley Way my legs felt like jelly and I had such a lump in my throat when I got to my seat I couldn't sing the National Anthem. Then when Neil actually scored a goal in England's 8–0 demolition of the Turks that evening I had to wipe away a tear. There he was playing alongside the likes of Bryan Robson, Peter Shilton and Gary Lineker – all players I had admired, well no, let's be honest about this, hero-worshipped and then after the match in the hospitality room, there I was standing shoulder to shoulder with them. Neil had felt this same sense of awe going down to breakfast on his first day of England training but everyone was very welcoming to the new boy. Gary Lineker even put his older statesman cap on, advising Neil on the agent dilemma. We had always thought we could do without one but now after becoming a fully fledged international Neil was approached to endorse a make of shin pad and a sum of money had been offered. How could we possibly know if this was a fair rate or how long the deal should last? Not that we hadn't experienced some, how shall we say, cold calling from various agents offering their wares. Indeed a phone call from a London-based adviser promised to make Neil a millionaire, while another arrived in his sports car brandishing a contract which it seemed entitled him to 20% of everything, down to our sons' pocket money.

Brian Clough detested the whole idea of agents. He just wanted to get on with the job of playing football and he was doing that so well at Forest that soon Neil was joined in the England squad by his colleagues Stuart Pearce, Steve Hodge, Des Walker and the manager's son Nigel. By 1989 Forest was a team to be reckoned with, winning the League Cup, and coming third in the league. Their progression to the semi-finals of the FA Cup – the only honour to elude Brian Clough – should also have been a moment to treasure. But that match against Liverpool at Hillsborough in April 1989 will sadly always be remembered not as a football match but as a national tragedy.

I lost a button from my shoe that day. Somewhere on the walk from the car to the ground it must have come loose. They were shiny, black shoes, flat with buttons on the side, like the shoes Sammy Davis Jnr wore to tap in those song and dance movies with Frank Sinatra and Dean

Martin. Big lavish Technicolor extravaganzas – you remember. I remember. I remember that day when thousands of ordinary football fans flocked in hope and anticipation to Hillsborough only for 96 of them to lose their lives – killed by incompetence and a lack of due care and regard for their safety. And now almost a decade since the tragedy the ordeal goes on for their families as they continue their fight for justice – and for the respect for their suffering that has so scandalously been denied them.

I was with my family that day. We had made the short drive up from Nottingham to Sheffield – my mum, dad, brother and his girlfriend. Neil's parents and his cousin. Whole families like us travelling to a big match just as footballing families had always done. In 1923, Neil's grandad George had been one of the thousands who took up literally what seemed to be an invitation from the FA to attend the first ever Cup Final at the newly built Empire Stadium in Wembley. He didn't have a ticket for the West Ham v. Bolton match but had gone to savour the atmosphere from outside the twin towers. But such was the confusion and volume of people that the gates were charged and walls torn down and George was carried inside. He took refuge from the crush on the pitch and was then pushed gently on to the touchline by George Scorey riding Billy, his grey hero of a horse. It was a miracle nobody was killed, and the judicial report which followed made recommendations for crowd safety as did another at the Burnden Park disaster at Bolton just after the Second World War. These reports were concerned with looking after the safety of the football fan but many of their recommendations were never implemented. Money and FA indifference seemed to be the primary reasons. How many fans' lives could have been saved at Burnden Park and Ibrox and Valley Parade and

Hillsborough had the concerns of the reports been addressed?

In April 1989 there was a carnival atmosphere as Forest fans drove up the M1 from Nottingham with seemingly every car bedecked with banners and scarves fluttering outside windows. We met up with Neil outside the players' entrance at the Hillsborough ground just after 2 p.m. He looked relaxed and Forest, already winners of the League Cup that season, looked like giving Liverpool more of a game than the previous year when they had lost to them at this ground at the same stage of the competition.

Perhaps it's some sort of psychological safety mechanism, that you recall not only the horror but also the more mundane incidents about the day. So that when my mum and I decided to visit the Ladies before getting settled, I remember we were pleasantly surprised at the obviously brand-spanking-new toilet facilities. As we emerged there was a Tannoy announcement: 'Would the fans in the Leppings Lane terraces behind the goal please move to the side pens as it's getting very unpleasant for the people at the front.' I looked up and could see a real crush developing behind the goal while there were hardly any fans in the side pens. Glancing at my watch I saw it was half past two – 30 minutes before kick-off and the fatal decision to open the Leppings Lane stand entrance to the fans who were in the crush outside. All that sophisticated equipment, all those cameras recording every detail of the escalating confusion, all those policemen on horseback and on foot who must have been desperately trying to convince their superiors of the seriousness of the problem on the ground. 96 people died because those superiors weren't listening. Why? The answer can be traced back to my experiences in Doncaster where public control was deemed much more important than public safety. The commanding officers at Hillsborough saw the growing crush but could not equate this with a danger to the well-being of the men, women and children in the Leppings Lane end. Indeed I believe the crowd became an amorphous entity, an enemy. The police knew what was going on and their inability to deal with it led to all that needless loss of life.

I realised something was seriously wrong when Liverpool fans started to climb over the fences at the front of the pen. I remember saying to my mum that the crush must be bad, for them to do that and risk arrest and ejection from the ground. In fact on the first few occasions the police on duty behind the goal shoved them back into the pen. 'Bloody hooligans,' a bloke in front of me shouted. But then fans at the back of the terracing began to be hauled up by those in the upper tier. The gates were opened, the match got under way, Peter Beardsley went on the attack for Liverpool and the roar went up . . .

Over the fences they came, tumbling on to the pitch. Soon it was covered with dazed people trying to come to terms with what was happening – that fans were dying in the tunnel and on the terracing. The referee stopped the game and the players returned to the dressing room where Neil sat hopelessly until around 7 p.m. He recalls how the players initially thought it was crowd trouble and that they'd soon be back on the pitch. It was only when they heard of the decision to use the gym as a temporary morgue that they realised the gravity of the situation. But in a surreal chilling few hours my mum and I, my brother and my dad witnessed it all. The most haunting image was when a young boy, maybe 11 or 12, was carried out of the bedlam and on to the pitch below us. His body was limp but his rescuer worked long and hard to save him, giving him mouth-to-mouth and massaging his chest. A huge involuntary cheer went up as the child seemed to cough and he was carried off to the ambulances we could hear arriving. Did that Liverpool youngster make it? I'll never know and I'll never be able to tell his mother how hard a fellow fan fought to save his life.

All we could do was stand and stare, bewildered by the chaos unfolding beneath us. The response from the police was farcical and the shocking contempt for the welfare of the ordinary fan has hung heavy over that day ever since. Since the Taylor Report the football industry has been transformed and the FA will tell you that the Hillsborough disaster is part of the bad, old days. Perhaps if the South Yorkshire Police had immediately admitted its culpability and apologised and, more importantly, if the relatives of the dead had been adequately compensated there would be some truth in this, but as we saw from Jimmy McGovern's docu-drama *Hillsborough* the appalling treatment of the relatives which began on the very day of the disaster has persisted over nearly a decade.

After the screening of *Hillsborough* I was haunted by the fact that our response at Nottingham Forest – flowers, a church service, donations – wasn't enough. I suppose that because Lord Justice Taylor was solving the problems of football's infrastructure I just assumed, with my faith in British justice, that the bereaved families were being treated fairly and with compassion. But as McGovern's documentary revealed, they faced hostility and disdain from almost everyone in authority they encountered. I have never been back to Hillsborough and until justice is done, I never will.

Alex Ferguson gestured to the photograph of Sir Matt Busby and his European Cup winning team of 1968. 'We're hamstrung by history,' he murmured more to

himself than to Neil and me. The moment passed and we
continued the Grand Tour, of the grandest ground of
them all – Old Trafford. Now almost a decade later
Manchester United's exciting, ebullient team of Fergie
Babes is surely just a quality player or two short of
conquering Europe and it is difficult to imagine the
extreme pressure facing Ferguson that summer of 1989.
Of course the manager had already tasted European success with Aberdeen but this was the big time. Promoted
from the provinces like some latter-day Roman senator,
Ferguson was the fledgling Caesar, faced with reawaken-
ing one of planet football's most famous sleeping giants.
Neil's stay at the club from 1989 to 1992 was at a time
when Ferguson was beset by the myriad problems of any
emerging dynasty as he fought to impose his own vision
and values. These turbulent years laid the groundwork
for all the success that has followed. Yet the 1989–90
season could easily have spelled an early end to
Ferguson's grand design. Had United not won the FA
Cup that year he might well have been sacked after
another poor performance in the league. But the Old
Trafford board held their nerve and gradually
Ferguson's undoubted genius as a manager prevailed.
Neil wasn't to be there to witness the final coming of age
of Ferguson's Manchester United. He was just one of the
casualties inevitable in such grand scheming but he – we
– would not have missed it for the world. It was a heady,
intoxicating time, a time which did not always bring out
the best in either of us as we both had to cope with the
pressures of being associated with a club adored by millions around the globe. But pass up the chance of playing
for the mighty Manchester United? Never.

So it was in the summer of 1989 we were being shown
around Old Trafford by Alex Ferguson. Neil was at that
time one of the most gifted midfield players in England.

His scoring prowess at Forest had brought him a strike rate of a goal every three games and he was an integral part of Bobby Robson's England team then involved in qualification for the World Cup being held in Italy the following year. Brian Clough, such an important influence in Neil's footballing development, wanted him to sign another contract with Forest and why not? We had always been very happy in Nottingham and had many friends there. But how could a player not fail to be flattered by an approach from Man United? Of course some disgruntled Forest fans put Neil's move down to baser motives. For ever after in fanzines such as *The Tricky Tree* he would be known as 'Fat Wallet Webb'. In fact he took a pay cut to go to Manchester United and if you'd only accompanied us on our Old Trafford tour that day you would have seen why. On first meeting Alex Ferguson I was struck by how young he looked, seemingly unaffected by the unimaginable pressures of football management, particularly at Manchester United. Ferguson was playing the congenial host that day but there was nothing he could do to disguise his Machiavellian detachment. Sir Matt Busby, who I was later to have the honour of meeting, ran his empire with an endearing paternalism. But football had changed and the pursuit of success as the nineties approached demanded more. It seemed this tall, handsome and proud Scot was better equipped than most.

A tiny exchange that day illustrates this single-mindedness. As we toured the restaurants and the executive boxes and walked out on to the hallowed turf I asked whether there was a crèche for the players' children. A friend at Aston Villa had just set one up and much maligned Millwall were planning one for the youngsters of their supporters. Oh no, I was informed. There just simply wasn't any room. No room in this huge coliseum but I remained silent. It was clear Old Trafford existed in Alex Ferguson's mind for two reasons only: first and most importantly for the pursuit of footballing immortality, and then to generate the millions of pounds necessary to sustain this pre-eminence. In marketing terms the Manchester United brand is a world leader and as we completed our tour that summer's day Luke, our three-year-old, was presented with a Manchester United teddy. 'What are you going to call it?' Ferguson asked. 'Forest,' came the reply.

Installed in a Sale hotel after United's pre-season tour to Thailand, Neil emptied yet another sackful of letters on to the hotel room coffee table. From Europe, Africa and the Far East, as well as from the city itself, huge numbers of Manchester United fans had put pen to paper to welcome their new player. Neil had always received a steady trickle of mail at his previous clubs. Most requested a signed photo and Neil would invariably include a letter. But this was something else. It was just as well that I was taking a summer break after sitting my finals. For hours on end we sat answering those letters and the aura that is inherent to Manchester United oozed from each and every one. Yet as well as the good will there was also a reminder of Neil's own personal responsibility. These fans were investing a great deal of their lives and money in the name of Manchester United. Yes, Neil Webb was one of the chosen few and as such would be revered but in return total loyalty and commitment was demanded. It had a Faustian feel about it – particularly in light of subsequent events. But even in Neil's darkest days at Old Trafford it is a great satisfaction to me that he never lost the support of the fans. Right to the bitter end he was receiving letters of encouragement.

Neil's league début for Manchester United was on the opening day of the 1989–90 season. The fixture list couldn't have thrown up a more attractive match – at home to Arsenal, the League Champions who had snatched the title so thrillingly from Liverpool on the last day of the previous season. Yet as I turned to the back pages of the newspapers expecting headlines hyping the tasty tie I was assailed by the shock news that Martin Edwards, the Manchester United chairman, was going to sell his stake in the club to a Michael Knighton. This had come completely out of the blue and as we got ready to drive to Old Trafford we wondered what the mystery investor had in mind to take the club forward. However, the intrigues at board level were soon forgotten as we got nearer Manchester's theatre of dreams. It was midday, almost three hours before kick-off but the huge sense of excitement and expectation was palpable as the roads around the ground teemed with fans. My personal challenge that day was just making it across the road from the car park, through the concourse and into the players' room. It seemed to take an age as Neil signed autographs, shook hands, had his picture taken and was generally hailed as the new hero.

Meanwhile I felt very uncomfortable as I was scrutinised from all angles. How glad I was to have toddler Luke sleeping in my arms. He deflected a certain amount of attention. Actually everyone was very welcoming and kind. I just felt very exposed and however much I told myself it was ridiculous, this interaction over the coming months and years became more and more of an ordeal. Yet I loved football fans: for goodness sake I was one. I knew what a thrill it would have been to meet my Chelsea heroes. But this was different. I wasn't Neil Webb, but as his wife I was part of the package – just as at the Hollywood Oscars we strain to see exactly who the adored stars are escorting up the famous red carpet. And so my obsession with looking the part began. So that unlike my days at Reading, Pompey and Forest when I would throw on a pair of jeans and a sweatshirt, now I started to dress up for the game, to have my hair done, to wear contact lenses instead of my glasses and generally to turn my nose up at anything that wasn't a designer label. Yet it wasn't done with any conviction or method, or indeed talent, so what resulted was a fashion disaster. If Neil was Old Trafford royalty then I was his Fool – dressed for gaudy effect but without any of the attendant's wit and irony. There was no joy in the fact I could go brandishing my credit card. The women who fussed over my hemline before swiping my card unnerved me almost as much as the Old Trafford crossing and I'd find myself going for weeks without buying a thing and then throwing myself into one afternoon of gross fashion gluttony, often just grabbing a handful of garments without even trying them on. It was little wonder I was a sartorial nightmare. I wore clothes that would look dated on my mother, others that would not go amiss round the back of King's Cross with gold bits and bobs randomly attached. Of course I felt wonderful, protected behind the traditional façade of the 'football wife'. But looking back I am horrified. The more important the game, the more outlandish the outfit. The European Cup Winners' Cup final in Rotterdam was my lowest point. King Midas would have rejoiced as I displayed an all-cream jean trouser suit, trimmed with gold braid and mother-of-pearl buttons encased in the fake precious metal. Alchemists would have swooned at my matching champagne belt and the *pièce de résistance* – metallic gold booties. How the chic Barcelona wives must have been sniggering through their sangria at the sight of me. The Spanish club may have lost to Manchester United that evening by two goals to nil but Catalan pride was restored with an easy fashion victory.

Of course, if somebody on that opening day of the season had informed me of the ludicrous siege mentality being a Manchester United wife was to induce, I would have thought 'What? Normal, well-adjusted me – never.' Indeed as kick-off drew near on Neil's début day, I was thankful for my flat shoes and old, comfy jeans as I struggled up to my allocated seat in the stand carrying Luke and the assorted paraphernalia designed to keep him occupied so I could watch the game in peace. A novel sideshow served to perplex and entertain us in equal measure as Michael Knighton, the new Manchester United 'owner', ran on to the pitch in shorts and sweatshirt, dribbling a ball. He then proceeded to perform a few keepie-uppies and score at the Stretford End. There was some cheering and not a little jeering which was probably more inspired by envy than concern for the club. After all, wasn't it every Manchester United fan's dream to take to the pitch and hit the back of the net? Of course Knighton never did take over the club but mysteriously remained as a non-executive director for several seasons until moving to Carlisle where he now holds a variety of posts, including that of chairman.

From the support act to what we'd all come to see, and Manchester United didn't disappoint. But in the light of my crèche request it was typical that I was scrabbling around under my seat looking for Luke's crayons when Neil followed Mr Knighton's lead by scoring from a thunderous volley. I looked up to see him salute the ecstatic Stretford End and then pointedly repeat the gesture to the bench. I'll always remember that look – a combination of gratitude to the manager and a pledge to repay the faith – because the euphoria was short-lived. Two weeks later Neil snapped his Achilles tendon playing for England. Things would never be quite the same again.

The club had provided us with a beautiful 200-year-old cottage in south Manchester. It was opposite Sunbank Wood where Neil would put in his extra training runs with Rosie and Pumpkin, our golden retrievers. However, the cottage, which we hoped to buy, was in need of substantial refurbishment and so we employed a builder, introduced to us by Alex Ferguson. Meanwhile we found rented accommodation in Wilmslow which, because we wanted to have the dogs with us, turned out to be less than adequate. In fact it was flea infested and we had to have it fumigated. Neil, though, had other things on his mind – England's vital World Cup qualifying match in Sweden. I was by now pregnant with my second son and stayed at home to watch the match on the TV. It was extremely eventful with Terry Butcher soldiering on with a bloody head wound and Neil dropping further back to help him out. But he was on the attack when he tried a shot at goal and without warning crumpled into a heap, clutching his leg. Over the years I had learned to be stoical about such things. Once at Portsmouth Neil had been knocked out and taken to hospital for a routine check. All he could remember was the snooker he'd watched the previous evening. Still, although he'd sustained his fair share of bruises and dead legs he'd never had a really serious injury. But now I watched as Neil was stretchered off the pitch. I spent a restless night waiting in vain for the phone to ring. The morning papers suggested it was an Achilles problem. I vaguely recalled that Neil's father Doug, also a professional footballer for a decade with Reading, had suffered a similar injury. My phone vigil continued until early afternoon when Neil finally rang and explained, in a voice close to tears, that he had shredded his Achilles tendon and was due to have an operation in a few hours. He would probably be out for at least the rest of the season

. . . and after that? – the threat to his career was left hanging over the phone line, unspoken. I would have to wait for another 24 hours before I could see him. Indeed Alex Ferguson visited my husband before me. Neil recalls there were tears of exasperation in the manager's eyes when he learned the extent of the injury. However, his midfield problem was soon solved with the speedy purchase of Paul Ince. I was left to pick up the pieces of Neil.

With his leg in plaster from hip to toe we set up a sun lounger in the sitting room of the rented house. He was a desperately depressed convalescent and, plagued by morning sickness which was of the all-day variety I found it difficult to be cheerful. The club did send their chaplain round for a chat but with hindsight a psychologist would have perhaps been more use as Neil's despair enveloped us. Martin Edwards, the United chairman did try to keep him in touch by inviting Neil as his guest in the directors' box at Maine Road. Unfortunately that was less than successful – it was United's infamous 5–1 defeat by local rivals Manchester City. Thank heavens for our wonderful neighbours who kept me sane during the long months of rehabilitation, as well as all the letters from around the world, and though I often used to leave the washing machine silent for a bit of company in the launderette, things slowly improved.

Our second son Josh was born in February 1990 and miraculously in April – seven months after his injury – Neil was close to match fit. Despite the early promise of the opening game against Arsenal, United's league form had been abysmal that season as Ferguson struggled to gel the undoubted talent he had assembled into a match-winning side. But they had had a great cup run and Neil, despite the fact that it was maybe a few weeks too soon, was happy to be playing his comeback game in a thrilling encounter with Oldham in the semi-final of the FA Cup.

We couldn't believe it. What a season. After all that heart-break, it looked like Neil was going to play in an FA Cup Final.

After Nottingham Forest beat Everton to win the Simod Cup at Wembley the players won a £10 bonus each and there was no party. Fair enough, some said, it was only a Mickey Mouse competition to fill the void caused by the ban on playing in Europe after the Heysel tragedy. But again we had to arrange our own party after Forest's League Cup win. What a contrast with Manchester United where not only the players and their families but all the staff from Old Trafford put on their glad rags to join the party heading south. FA Cup Final day was magical. The Crystal Palace faithful let off hundreds of balloons and the goals flowed as Ian Wright came off the bench to grab two for Palace and Mark 'Sparky' Hughes saved Man U with another brace. After extra time the final score was 3–3, a fantastic match for the neutral but I felt emotionally wiped out and we all had to go back and do it again. The replay was a much more dour affair but suddenly a long, telling pass from Neil in midfield found Lee Martin running into the area and amazingly the left back scored the winning goal. I'll never forget Archie Knox, then Alex Ferguson's assistant, spraying everyone with champagne on the train home and singing his way through a Manchester United dream team: 'And number one was Georgie Best and number two was Georgie Best and number three was Lee Martin, and number four was Georgie Best. . .' I think Bryan Robson may have got a look-in at number seven.

Before we'd had time to really savour the FA Cup Final the World Cup was looming. Neil had rushed back into the Manchester United team because Ferguson needed him and it had paid off handsomely. Now the England manager Bobby Robson was granting him the ultimate accolade in any footballer's career: the chance to go to the World Cup Finals. Robson was a well-liked manager and had the respect of all the players and definitely that of the players' wives when he invited us all on a week's holiday in Sardinia at England's World Cup headquarters. We met up in a hotel in Luton and it was here I encountered Paul Gascoigne for the first time. He was like a kid breaking up for the summer holidays and it wasn't too much of a surprise when he discovered he'd forgotten his passport. Fortunately his bosom buddy Jimmy Five Bellies was on hand to make the long drive back to Newcastle and Paul and Neil bedded in at the hotel bar to wait for him. My part in the vigil only lasted until 1 a.m. but I had a taste of the goldfish bowl that 'Gazza' has lived his life in ever since, as the tabloids the next morning told a scurrilous tale of boozy high jinks when in reality we were just a small group of people having a drink in a hotel bar.

During the holiday Paul, one of the few players who didn't bring a partner, played the Just William role, generally keeping us all amused but once or twice going too far, like trying to capsize a trio of wives on a pedalo. But at least it gave the gun-toting, rubber-clad security guards a laugh. They weren't so amused though when Paul, pedalling like mad, made a break for it out of the bay and they pursued him in their 007-style dinghy. Paul was like a breath of fresh air and just a week before I was writing this, nearly a decade later, he approached Neil at a testimonial match to thank him, as he always does, for giving him his first chance to shine in England's midfield: 'Webby, lad, thanks for getting injured in 1989 . . .'

The Sardinian base was an idyllic one. Only ten weeks after giving birth to Josh I kept well covered up but as you can imagine there were plenty of beautiful bodies floating around as well as the spying eye of the paparazzi lenses.

The pickings were poor and they were getting desperate so finally they went for a photo of Bobby Robson apparently paying too close attention to Mrs Gary Stevens, a player's wife blessed with model-like proportions. That wasn't enough, though, so they moved on from manipulating camera angles to personnel in the players' complex. Witness the forlorn phone call I took at 3 a.m. in the morning from Neil just a week after I'd returned home. 'It's lies, all lies, tell the other wives,' he mumbled. I just put it down to too much sun or another late night with Mr Gascoigne and went back to sleep. So boy was I in for a shock when I read in one of the tabloids the next day that 'Isabella, the sexy Italian siren' was claiming she had been taught the art of England's foreplay by a trio from the squad. Actually the woman in question, a receptionist at the hotel, had been completely misquoted and had to go into hiding to escape the snarling press pack. It was rumoured Stuart Pearce was one of the trio. Do me a favour. If I know Stuart, he would have run a mile from the lovely Isabella, probably believing she was some kind of Mata Hari trying to get tactical secrets.

I was sitting with Liz, Stuart's wife, high in the gods of the Stadio delle Alpe in Turin on the evening of the Italia 90 semi-final when England took on West Germany. The seats were awful – all 25 million of you back in Blighty got a better view than us but we weren't ungrateful. The FA had flown us to Turin free of charge to see the team take on the mighty Germans. Neil, as expected after his long lay-off, had been a squad member only and as the team progressed through the tournament I caught glimpses of him on TV perched on flowerpots as there was no room on the bench. Any footballer's wife will tell you it is always a difficult thing when your man is not involved. Of course you want the team to win. Of course you give your full support. But – and I have to admit it –

when Paul Gascoigne was booked during the semi-final, subsequently disqualifying himself from the final should England win, you may have wept buckets with him but I was looking on the bright side. Steve McMahon would probably replace Paul and that would mean Neil had a good chance of being a substitute if the team made it through. A World Cup Final . . . But there was extra time to get through and as the minutes ticked away Liz Pearce became more and more solemn. 'I don't want Stuart to take a penalty,' she kept muttering to herself. I thought it was some sort of psychological prop – I'd never seen Stuart miss a spot kick. When he did, I cried. I cried for them both because I knew how Liz must feel and when Chris Waddle ballooned his penalty over the bar I cried for Neil too. He was never going to play in a World Cup Final. After we'd calmed down we decided to go round to the players' changing room to lend a bit of moral support. But as we approached the tunnel entrance, we were stopped by a gun-toting Italian guard who shooed us away: 'Go away, you English groupies.' Later we discovered that Stuart's number had come up for a random drug test. The long game and subsequent dehydration had left him unable to give a sample. His German counterpart had the same problem. So with the rest of the team on the bus desperate to get away from the scene of their defeat, Stuart had to sit in the same room as his vanquisher, waiting, waiting . . .

If England was in despair it was nothing compared to the mourning of the Italian nation who had also been dumped out in the semi-finals. So the third place play-off in Bologna was a sombre affair although at least Neil came on as a second-half substitute and he even hit the post. A World Cup medal and a raucous plane journey home lifted the spirits. There was to be a welcoming committee at Luton airport. No room for the wives, though.

While the players were to ride in an open-topped bus we were to be sent on ahead to the hotel in a coach to pick up our cars.

Any peevishness we might have initially felt about this separation was soon forgotten as we were over-whelmed by the tumultuous welcome at the airport. Thousands of fans had come to hail their heroes. 'Get your tits out for the lads,' a chorus sang as we climbed on to the coach. We looked up to see where the cheeky invitation was coming from and saw hundreds of fans on the roof of the arrivals building. Lampposts were similarly occupied, as was the roof of the nearby petrol station which looked like it might not stand up to the strain of the close-to-delirious fans. But we were just a sideshow. Wearing a pair of plastic bosoms, Paul Gascoigne, the man whose tears had well and truly brought football home, was the star attraction as the bus wound its way out of the airport. It took us all hours to reach the hotel. Not that we minded. It was a wonderful sight and a fitting tribute to our glorious national game.

With such a fairy-tale ending to the season it was perhaps almost inevitable that there would be some payback for Neil's precipitous rush back to action and the 1990–91 season was mainly a dreadful one in terms of his performance on the pitch. The sparkle went out of his game as bad form followed niggling injuries and bad luck. I recall one particular time when he'd returned from yet another setback and had played a decent game at last. After three minutes of the next week's match at Sheffield United he found three of his ribs at the end of Vinny Jones's elbow as he went in for a 50-50 tackle. The ribs still give him trouble now when he laughs or picks up the children. Mr Jones put his head around the Man Utd dressing-room door after the match to profess no hard feelings – as you can imagine, my sentiments at the time weren't quite so charitable. Indeed, it was an especially difficult time for me as our baby Josh was often in and out of hospital with chronic asthma.

Neil's unhappiness was all consuming. He had a stinker during the 1991 League Cup Final defeat against Sheffield Wednesday and knew he was probably out of contention for the European Cup Winners' Cup match against Barcelona. I did feel shut out. But churlishness is not part of my make-up so I put on a smile – and the aforementioned gold jean suit disaster – and headed for Rotterdam. Actually, I'm glad I did as for the first and only time in my 'career' as a football wife I got a decent seat. It was soft and expansive like a first-class airline seat and it was in with all the top brass. Neil also got the best seat he could hope for: after recovering from yet another setback he was on the bench and so in line for a medal should Manchester United win. Which they did, thanks to the splendid star that is Sparky Hughes. A quiet, humble man off the pitch with an equally lovely family, Mark is truly one of the great players of the modern era and the fact that he subsequently came to play for Chelsea has absolutely no bearing on this neutral judgement at all . . .

That evening was a wonderful night of celebration in a hotel outside Rotterdam. Along with Lee Sharpe and new signing Andrei Kanchelskis, who couldn't speak a word of English, I think I was the last one to leave the dance floor. Of course this was more than Manchester United's triumph. It was the final stage of England's rehabilitation back into the European fold.

The following evening we flew back to Manchester. For months I'd been looking at my tickets for the concert Luciano Pavarotti was giving at Manchester's cavernous G-Mex and cherishing them – well, at £90 a head you had to treat them with a certain respect. But our flight was delayed and as Neil had to take part in the celebratory coach ride through the city, I went alone. Pavarotti, ever the populist, once again judged the mood and donned, to what seemed like universal approval – Manchester City fans must have had to bite their tongues – a Manchester United cap and scarf to sing 'Nessun Dorma' for his finale. I cried and cried. The tears were still gushing out uncontrollably as I sat alone in the huge auditorium long after everyone had gone . . .

After the European Cup Winners' Cup win I went on the offensive. Neil's injuries and recent poor performances had taken their toll and he needed help to get his confidence back. So I engaged a sports psychologist to devise a summer programme. But Neil also had to help himself, and that meant a complete revision of his lifestyle. Out went the steak and chips and in came pasta and rice. The drinking was cut out completely. Neil had always enjoyed a drink. It was part of the football culture, and in moderation it is important for team building and morale. However, Neil was starting to use it as an escape. A year to the day that Neil suffered his Achilles ankle injury he sat morosely at home and got very drunk. I thought I'd leave him alone to sleep it off and tackle him about it the next day. I was drifting in and out of sleep, rehearsing what I was going to say to him in the morning, when I became aware that the house had been quiet for a very long time. With a sudden but overwhelming sense of foreboding I went looking for him. I needn't have worried. I found him in the dining room relieving himself into a cut-glass decanter. I went ballistic, which wasn't a good idea as he was sleepwalking and came to, a gibbering wreck. When we both calmed down he explained he'd dreamt he was still in hospital and was using the urine bottle . . .

Thankfully in the summer of 1991 Neil took a much

more holistic approach to his life and fitness and even I was amazed at his rejuvenation as the season began. Man of the Match and of the Month: awards from the tabloids began to roll in that autumn – by a fortunate coincidence one of them came with a Waterford cut-glass decanter – and the following spring, I'll never forget the day Neil declared that he was finally back to his best. It came after a packed Old Trafford crowd had watched Man U put in a scintillating League Cup display against Middlesbrough. Neil's return to form had not gone unnoticed on the international front either and his rehabilitation seemed complete when he was recalled to the England team, now under the auspices of Graham Taylor, for a friendly against France. It had been a long, hard haul but at last we could relax and enjoy the return to footballing success. How naive we were to think that life was that simple and how we underestimated the enormous pressure that Alex Ferguson was under. At Christmas it seemed that the League title that had eluded them for so long was there for the taking. United were ten points clear and walking on air. But it was a team that was vulnerable in two areas – loss of confidence in the face of pressure and a distinct lack of depth outside the small squad of top calibre players – and during the run-in these fault lines began to show. Alex Ferguson started chopping and changing a winning team. It was painfully inevitable that nerves began to jangle as the pressure increased and the players became somewhat bewildered. Neil found himself dropped for the Sheffield United game after jokingly saying in the dressing room the week prior to the match that he hadn't had a kick in the last game against them. He was devastated and all the old doubts came back to haunt him. Somehow Manchester United lost their way and as the season began to wane the results became more and more erratic. The failure of Alex

Ferguson to hold his nerve lost the club the title that year, and Neil his career.

The team regrouped for the 1992–93 season and after the inspired signing of Eric Cantona, Manchester United dominated domestic football for the next five years. Neil was clearly not part of Alex Ferguson's game plan. He washed his hands of a player he believed had let the side down. Neil's crime? Wanting to play for England.

It was as the race for the championship began to gather pace that Graham Taylor requested Neil's presence for a friendly in Czechoslovakia. With England already assured of a place at the European Championships to be held in Sweden that summer Taylor was now using these final warm-up matches to select his squad. There were also call-ups for the other internationals at Old Trafford but the rumour went round the Man United dressing room that Ferguson didn't want his players to go. With hindsight it is easy to understand the manager's concern. He was struggling to hold Manchester United's title challenge together. The last thing he wanted was half his team going off for several days with all the attendant risk of injury. But instead of calling Neil into his office to explain the situation Ferguson remained silent.

If only – yes, I know, we're not allowed 'if onlys', but if I can have just one – if only Alex Ferguson had taken Neil aside and explained how he felt. But the first Neil really understood about Ferguson's strength of feeling was when he was substituted during the last 20 minutes of a match against Wimbledon. I had left my mother at home looking after the children and knowing that she would be listening on the radio I gave her a quick call to reassure her that Neil wasn't injured. After the match the physio informed Neil he was going to ring Graham Taylor and tell him he had picked up an injury and couldn't join the England squad. Manchester United paid his wages so, though it broke his heart, he had no choice. Meanwhile fate had conspired against him as Graham Taylor had phoned our home after hearing about Neil's 'injury' from a journalist. 'No,' my mother declared. 'Shelley's just rung. He's perfectly OK.' There then followed an almighty row between Taylor and Ferguson with accusations of sabotage and lack of fair play flying around – what fun the tabloids had. In international terms the upshot was a new decree from FA headquarters that withdrawals had to be substantiated with a doctor's certificate. Alex Ferguson never forgave Neil.

There then followed a bizarre situation. Neil was dropped for the last few vital games of Man Utd's season but then discovered he was part of Graham Taylor's England squad for the European Championships. He didn't make the team for the first two group matches, both soulless draws, but then earned a place in the England midfield for the crucial third and final game against the hosts, Sweden. And where was I at kick-off? In the middle of my dress rehearsal for *The Taming of the Shrew* in deepest Cheshire. I'd concealed my personal stereo pretty well in the deep pockets of my Elizabethan dress and my headphones were safely tucked away beneath my snood. Even so I nearly missed my entrance in Act I when England went 1–0 up. But just as Kate hurled Petruchio into the fountain so England's dreams were drenched as Tomas Brolin added to Dahlin's early second-half strike. Another dream was over but not before, in a scene reminiscent of any big screen epic, the only Englishman (Sparky's Welsh) who you would entrust to turn the tide back our way, Gary Lineker, was substituted and the result stood for ever clothed in tabloid infamy: Swedes 2, Turnips 1.

Intrinsically, a footballer is a commodity. When he is

surplus to requirements he is shipped out. It is painful but the humiliation of staying on at United was worse. Apart from twenty minutes on as a substitute against Ipswich when he got a tremendous reception and hit the post, Neil's last few months at Old Trafford at the start of the 1992–93 season were a slow torture. His tenure had already degenerated into farce when he was sent home from an away trip to Southampton. I had dropped Neil off to catch the team coach one Sunday teatime – they were playing the Saints on the Monday night. We had shared a bottle of wine over lunch, toasting each other with yet another hope for an upturn in our fortunes. How ironic then that Ferguson, checking in on arrival at the hotel got a whiff of our tentative celebration and sent Neil home for being 'drunk'. He was fined two weeks' wages but negotiations with the Professional Footballers' Association and Gordon Taylor reduced this to one. How I wish now I'd made a fuss about this and insisted that the money go to charity rather than to the club's coffers already overflowing with surplus cash. But there was not even this scant consolation as the weeks of being ostracised turned to months. We were completely helpless. It was a ludicrous and excruciatingly painful time. Then we heard that Nottingham Forest, floundering near the bottom of the newly created Premiership, were interested in having their old boy back – but at the right price. Impasse. Ferguson didn't want to play him but he didn't seem to want to let him go either. It was driving me nuts. Then suddenly I had the ammunition in my hands to precipitate matters. It was a huge gamble and one I'm not particularly proud of but I suppose it did the trick. I had just started my first television work for a BBC2 football fanzine show, *Standing Room Only*. It was a great programme to work on as each week I could review the gossip, tackle fans' problems and mull over the latest football publications. One week I was presented with Alex Ferguson's book about his first six years at Manchester United. Yes there were derogatory references to Neil and yes I felt they were unjustified but it wasn't just on a personal level that I felt uncomfortable with the book. Players who had chosen not to sign for Manchester United were referred to with heavy sarcasm and those who had their share of problems and had departed during Ferguson's early tenure were vilified. I discussed it with Neil and the next night stood in front of a television camera and said what I thought. The manager knew nothing about this attack until he walked into the Cliff training ground the next day and was shown the back page of the *Daily Mirror*. TROUBLE AND STRIFE ATTACK I believe the headline ran. Apparently Mr Ferguson was incandescent with rage and shortly afterwards he sold Neil for £800,000 to Forest. Mission accomplished.

There was one small matter for our agent Jon Holmes to finalise – our beautiful Rose Cottage transformed by the efforts of Alex Ferguson's builder. It was a club house but we were responsible for any improvements above and beyond a certain level. Our bank balance was being drained by the work, so much so that towards the summer of 1990 I began to get suspicious. My father, who became a builder himself when he finished in football, advised me to seek independent advice but as this was a delicate matter involving a friend of the United manager, I approached Maurice Watkins, one of the club directors who many regard as the power behind the throne in the development of Manchester United. He was courtesy personified and acted promptly, appointing an independent surveyor to look into my concern. Such deliberations take months but by the time things began to sour on the field of play it was clear we had been overcharged by something in the region of £10,000. Now we were faced with a long and costly legal procedure to recover the money – that is, unless Manchester United footed the bill. After all, Rose Cottage was a club house that we had hoped to buy at some stage. Martin Edwards, the chairman could see the logic of this. But there was one proviso: we were not in any circumstances to tell Alex Ferguson.

The Nottingham Forest Christmas party was well under way when I arrived at the City Ground after a frosty journey over the Peaks from Manchester. I'd said goodbye to Rose Cottage, now liberated of such cloying adornments as a fitted kitchen, a bath and two toilets – compensation for the strain of finding we had been diddled and the sweetest revenge. It was a poignant moment but I shoved hot bendy rollers tightly into my hair as a distraction and set off. After a two-hour journey I arrived at the Nottingham hotel where the club was putting us up until we found somewhere to live and I remembered the bendies. It was too late – I looked like a clown so I tied the frizzy disaster into a pink bow which of course matched my party frock, a tasteful little number with candy petticoats and a matching bolero jacket trimmed with pearls. I'm surprised the hotel receptionist didn't have me arrested for impersonating a Knickerbocker Glory. I wobbled out to the car in my pink strappy sandals and made the Forest do just in time for the mince pies. It was great to be back with people I had known so well and I danced with furious abandon until, exhausted, I flopped down at a table next to the dance floor. 'Shelley,' drawled a laconic Irish voice. 'It's not a bloody fancy dress, you know.' Roy Keane, then still at Nottingham Forest and usually Mr Reticent, had suddenly encapsulated the last three years of my life. I'd been living in some kind of fantasy world with definite delusions of grandeur. Why else do I have to this day a cupboard full of shoes, all in their boxes, all unworn? (What is this link between compulsive shoe acquisition and unpleasant women? Someone should do a Ph.D. on it.) It was just grotesque how smug I had become.

In fact, another footballer had identified the degeneration as long ago as the FA Cup Final in 1990. We were on our way back to Manchester from Wembley on a lovely old Pullman train the day after the drawn first match against Crystal Palace and we were playing a game. Viv Anderson, always the team ringmaster, was writing down names of famous people and sticking them on everyone's back. We then had to guess what our celebrity identity was. My turn came. Am I a film star? 'She thinks she is,' chuckled Viv. A royal? A politician? A television personality? All elicited the same response. Finally the look in Viv's eye brought me to my senses. He'd written 'Shelley Webb'. How I laughed with them through my discomfort. How lucky I thought I'd been, but it was all a façade. We'd become Charles Dickens's Veneerings, our lives all artifice and superficiality as the family homage to Neil's career had consumed everything else that was decent. A Granada crew once came to film at Rose Cottage for a home-improvement programme. I was showing the presenter around upstairs when she opened the door to my study, the room where I had chucked all the clutter which was preventing the house from being perfect that day. 'Don't go in there!' came my shrill cry. In that room was my family, the real us, only I just couldn't see it or how important it was to us. Years later when I eventually struggled free of the smugness and tried to release the pause button on my own life I found the whole world was falling apart. And the greatest irony of all was that during this period when it may have appeared I was revelling in my new glamorous role I was in fact desperately unhappy.

Coming home to Nottingham Forest, to Brian Clough who hated anything or anyone remotely 'starry' was supposed to be a cleansing process. It could have been, but Neil's childlike pleasure at returning to his old club was soon replaced by another long struggle back from injury as the Achilles tendon on his other leg snapped and he could only watch helplessly as Forest were relegated to the first division in the summer of 1993. It was an ignominious end to Brian Clough's rich and fruitful career. A new regime was installed the following season and Frank Clark, a famous Forest old boy, decided Neil's injury had impaired his mobility irreparably. As far as the new manager was concerned Neil was yesterday's man and nothing could persuade him otherwise. So when Neil came off the bench in a cup game against Manchester City to score the equaliser and set up the winner it still wasn't enough to win him a recall.

This final rejection hung gloomily over the household. Neil had put on a lot of weight while recuperating and, rather like a woman after one too many pregnancies, he was finding it difficult to shed. The familiar chant from the Forest faithful of 'Who ate all the pies?' was now replaced with cries of 'Mr Blobby'. Neil had always had a good rapport with the crowd and played along with them, lifting his shirt and rubbing his belly. Of course the fans appreciated his ability to laugh at himself but I don't think Neil was laughing that hard. He became obsessed with losing weight. He'd eat nothing all day and then I'd wake in the middle of the night to hear him maniacally riding the exercise bike, and that on top of training and afternoon gym visits. He lost weight but at one point I thought he was losing his mind, particularly as Forest's return to the Premiership the following season resulted in relegation for Neil out of the first-team squad into the 'stiffs'. It was the last year of his contract and I diligently watched every reserve match: a weird combination of players like Neil coming to the end of their career, youngsters hoping to impress to get that elusive professional contract and those out of favour. A distinctly depressing experience when we knew the only way out was down and out. But then, out of the blue, Neil got a call to go on loan to Hong Kong for a couple of months. It seemed like a great idea – going to the other side of the world because somebody wanted you. Actually I'd heard the standard there was modest to say the least and I had misgivings about him being out of sight of those managers from the lower divisions who might have welcomed the experience of a former international. But I said nothing because by this stage I wanted him to go away. I wanted the peace and quiet to mull over what I now knew to be a fact – that our marriage was in crisis. Neil's dedication to football was always an obsession and we all had to worship at the altar of his career. But now he began to exclude everybody. He trained all day long and hardly ate. He became monosyllabic and the children must have wondered why this morose man was living in their daddy's clothes. If it hadn't been for my work I dread to think what would have happened. At least when he was in Hong Kong the bad dreams stopped, particularly the one which always featured life insurance and a foolproof murder.

The tranquillity was short-lived. Neil returned after only five weeks with an injury and shortly after that the safety net of a regular wage disappeared as his contract expired. Frantic with worry I began to work a six-day week and finally, because I realised that I could get by without him, I told him he could leave if he didn't pull himself together. They were harsh words, particularly as I knew he was probably clinically depressed. But his refusal to even countenance the fact that he might have a problem forced my hand. Thankfully he did start to follow a sensible regime and indeed blossomed but that was probably more to do with the fact that the phone rang. Third division Exeter invited him down to Devon for a pre-season trial. The cobwebs in the players' wives' toilet at the other St James's Park and the jolly optimism of all involved with the struggling club was a breath of fresh air, and with hindsight Neil probably should have counted himself lucky and not taken up the challenge just before the start of the 96–97 season to try out for Grimsby. The first division side were then managed by Brian Laws, a former team-mate from Neil's Forest days. 'Come and join us on a week-to-week contract,' suggested Brian. 'We're at home to Wolves on the opening day of the season.'

It was a weird feeling making that journey up to Grimsby's home ground Blundell Park, as I had to so many grounds, so many years ago. During the last few years I'd realised that my feelings towards football had curdled. On a professional level it still dominated my life but I was weary of the demands it had made on us as a family, the price it had exacted. But as I chatted with the Wolves fans on the train my impoverished football spirit began to regenerate. I could feel the tears well up as Neil ran out on to the field to a rousing reception from the crowd. The day didn't go quite to plan. Steve Bull scored a hat trick for Wolves. But the 1–3 scoreline was misleading as Grimsby had shone in patches and Neil had set up their goal. He more than held his own at this level and obviously others agreed with me, as he was awarded the Grimsby Man of the Match champagne. Of course playing pretty football isn't enough and the results failed to come for Grimsby. Neil was released and Brian Laws sacked. Exeter understandably turned their backs and Neil descended into the purgatory that is non-league football, at Aldershot and then Weymouth.

I don't want to disparage the great grass roots of our national game but for a former England international playing at this level is soul destroying. Meanwhile I composed letter after letter on his behalf for jobs of every kind at football league clubs. Every now and again he would get an interview such as the one where he was drummed out of Blackpool for daring to suggest the Tangerine men might play with wing backs. Another time he thought he might be in the running for the Reading player-manager job, but to no avail.

How lonely I became. Self-awareness was no substitute for the loss of not only a husband and a father but a best friend. For even now after what I hoped was the road to recovery, the cloying shroud of Neil's footballing career was shutting us out again. This mourning had to stop. So we left him. The children and I walked away. It was a bombshell – of nuclear proportions but not part of some master recovery plan. When I left him I thought that that was it. I had had enough. Miraculously it seems to have changed him and slowly the pre-Manchester-United man has emerged. Now I can only think, why didn't I do it years ago? I suppose because I had to solve my own crisis of identity first, to emerge from my own make-believe football wife world.

Most evenings there's a mass gathering of the family on the threshold of the TV room as various radios and shouts of 'goal!!!' bring us running from all over the house to watch the action replay and argue over the merits of the attack and defence. Yes, football is still dominating our lives but it's back to the joyous way. Neil is now coaching youngsters and is forging a career in the sports media. There are still occasional bad days but we can now look ahead to the future with confidence that as a family we can face most things. Our boys are both huge football fans and I recall the geography teacher one parents' evening expressing her amazement at Luke's knowledge of European cities, although it was a little strange that he always referred to one German town as Borussia Dortmund. At six years old Luke decided he wanted to go to live in Rio de Janeiro so he could become a naturalised Brazilian and play for the national team. I told him they would never countenance anyone who only had a right foot. Now he plays for the Reading Schools Representative side and scores with his left as well. Young Josh supports Man Utd – well, he was born in Manchester and visited Old Trafford for the first time recently. The tickets came courtesy of the club – which I'm hoping is a sign they've forgiven me for relieving Rose Cottage of the odd toilet or two.

'That was the best day of my life,' smiled Josh, laden down with scarves and posters and a towel from the megastore. 'And d'you know when the next best day of my life will be?' I somehow had an inkling what the serious little voice was going to say: 'When I play for them . . .'

Denise Gallagher

Denise is married to Des, goalkeeper for Conference League side Stevenage Borough, who in 1998 took Newcastle United to a replay in the FA Cup. She is currently studying for a degree in psychology at Luton University.

Des and I had just split up when he did his streak across a local football club pitch. He was watching an Isthmian League game when he says he became momentarily deranged because we had finished, and suddenly took off all his clothes and started streaking. Isthmian League officials weren't very happy and they suspended him from playing for eight games. A decade later and the *Sun* actually wanted to pay him to do a full monty and it was all to do with Des's non-league team Stevenage Borough drawing Newcastle United from the Premiership in the FA Cup. We got so much publicity it was bizarre. It wasn't just that this was the part-time minnows against the big boys: there was also a lot of bad feeling between the two clubs, which of course the press loved, because although Stevenage had been drawn to play at home, Newcastle and their manager Kenny Dalglish felt that the match should be switched to their ground, St James's Park. Everybody loves an underdog and I think the Stevenage chairman Victor Green cleverly played on this. He wasn't going to be intimidated by Newcastle and he was adamant he wouldn't switch the game to the north-east. Of course he was helped by the money that satellite TV, obviously hoping for an upset, offered him for Stevenage to play at home.

It seemed everyone was interested in the game. Me and Des were interviewed on TV and every day another newspaper would be on the phone wanting to come and talk to us. It was like it wasn't really happening and of course I had to keep tidying the house. Then Des came home from training and said the *Sun* wanted to do a picture of him with only a football covering his private parts. I laughed: 'You're like a prostitute – you'll do anything for a few bob.'

In the end there was a full page of Des in the altogether and he did look good. In fact he didn't even have to take his underpants off – the photographer said just roll them up. Des works for the government assessing insulation grants for people on benefit so he has to travel around a lot and he started to get recognised on the underground and at hot-dog stands in London. He would take Calum and our other little boy Reuben up to school and the kids would be lining up in the playground to get his autograph. It was very sweet and he became a sort of local hero.

Calum and Reuben both came with me to watch the match at Stevenage and it was amazing because people in the crowd were pointing me out as Des's wife and making a fuss of the children. But to tell you the truth I was just looking at Alessandro Pistone, Newcastle's Italian defender running up and down, thinking, 'God, you're gorgeous.' I said to Des before the game: 'Just get Pistone's autograph.'

The England striker Alan Shearer had just come back from a long lay-off through injury but he showed his class by scoring first for Newcastle. I thought, that's it then, but amazingly we equalised and held on for a 1–1 draw. We couldn't believe it and I don't think the Newcastle players could either. Newcastle knew that this was the biggest game in the lives of the Stevenage players and once the final whistle and the contest was over they should have shown them some respect by perhaps having a drink with them in the bar afterwards.

Of course Stevenage were always going to be up against it at St James's Park for the replay. Des's brother runs a pub in Luton town centre and I went to watch the match on the big screen. It was an unbelievable atmosphere but I wish in a way we'd lived in Stevenage through all this, instead of Luton, because the whole town was united and rooting for the team. It put Stevenage on the map and it was a special time for everyone. Des told me that after they lost the replay the Stevenage lads went in the Newcastle players' bar but there wasn't much talk between the teams.

It makes me laugh when I remember that all through the first match Mark 'Smudger' Smith, who was marking Alan Shearer, was after his shirt. He was really winding Shearer up: 'Al, give us your shirt, give us your shirt' all the way through the match. Shearer was swearing at him that no one was going to have his shirt. Well, of course that upset a few of the lads but I must admit a couple of weeks later Shearer did send down two signed shirts to the club. However, I still don't think there was that much of a gap in the teams to justify the huge gulf in money between them. What I could do with just one week of their wages . . .

We used the money we earned from the Newcastle game to go on holiday to Australia and New Zealand. Des and I love both countries and have lived in Australia on two occasions over the years. We actually met when I was 21 and Des was 19. I'd seen him and quite fancied him from afar. One night my friend and I went to an Indian restaurant after going to Hatters, a nightclub in Luton. Des came in with his brother. Because it was busy Des's brother sat down next to me and Des beside my friend. I looked across the table at Des and I thought, 'I'm going to marry you.' I really did. He had such a beautiful face. I asked him what he did for a living. 'I'm a donkey,' he replied, which meant he was a labourer, but that didn't put me off.

Des went off to Germany to work with his brother.

Then one night my friend said: 'Guess who's back? Des.'
I thought, oh he'll have forgotten about me. But I had a
wedding to go to and he was there. He was so drunk that
when his brother picked him up on his shoulders they fell
over and landed in some sick. It didn't put me off. In fact
when I saw him at the bar I gave him a kiss. After that he
said he would ring me. 'Do you want me to ring you?' I
offered. I was so eager.

We came from the two big council estates in Luton and
Des played in goal for a local team. I used to get so embarrassed when I watched him play. I mean he was so quiet
off the pitch then I'd go and watch him on a Sunday and
he'd be yelling instructions at everyone because he was
the goalkeeper. He was real rough, telling everyone what
to do – not the guy I thought he was. But I was so besotted with Des that I'd go and watch him do anything.

I was a hairdresser at the time and I had just come
back from working a season in Jersey when we met. I'd
also spent time living on the beach in the Canaries and I
was planning to go off to America to get a nannying job.
But as soon as I saw Des I knew that was it. But I still had
this travelling bug and I wanted to go to Australia. So we
saved up for a year and then went off to Perth. Des
played for North Perth Croatia football team and while
he was there George Best came out for a guest appearance. Des did well with the team and we were there for a
year. It was great. We had a lovely house with a pool and
did wonderful things like swimming with dolphins.

But we came back to Luton, and that's when we split
up. Des was going to go abroad and buy a bar but then
his brother was injured in a stabbing and a close friend of
his died. Losing someone close to you makes you weigh
up your life: it brought us back together and we got married. When our first baby, Calum, was born I got post-
natal depression. We had a big mortgage and Des was

running his own fencing business so he was very busy. He then had a big operation on his knee and it all just became too much. I needed to escape. So we sold up again and moved to Melbourne and then on to the Gold Coast. Des began playing for the Gold Coast Gamblers team. It was run by John Charlton, the son of the former England international and Eire manager, Jack. I began training as a telephone counsellor for Lifeline and became interested in psychology. When we came back again to live in Luton I continued studying in this area.

Des played in goal for Dunstable for a while before Paul Fairclough, the Stevenage Borough manager, asked him to join his Conference team. I then began a course in neuro-linguistic programming at London's Regent's College. NLP is often used to help sports people excel in their field and Paul McKenna, the hypnotist, who has worked with boxers, is a NLP practitioner. After a while I decided to try out my new skills on Des. Stevenage were going through a sticky patch so one Friday night in bed, I told Des if he allowed me to take him through the NLP process then I was sure they would win the following day. Well, Stevenage got hammered and Des came home shouting: 'Don't you ever use that on me again.' Of course he needed to do more work than just the night before a game, and sports psychology is a growing field.

Stevenage missed out on promotion to the football league because their ground wasn't up to league stan-dards. It knocked the stuffing out of them and although they have now had the necessary work done on the ground they haven't been able to reach the same foot-balling level since. Des is in his mid-thirties now, in the twilight of his career, which is why the Newcastle match was so amazing. It was the biggest thing that ever hap-pened to him and it came so late. I can't help thinking, what would have happened if he'd been ten years younger? Would he have had the chance of joining a league team? He did once get a taste of the big time – as a stand-in for David Seaman, the England goalkeeper. Nike approached Des while they were filming their advert on Hackney Marshes because he and Seaman look quite alike – except Des is better looking, of course! They made him put on a false moustache but even so, when the ad appeared on TV Des was nowhere to be seen. He was the understudy in case Seaman got injured during filming – I'm sure Arsenal would have been pleased.

I dread the day when Des finishes playing football. Even though he has always been a part-time player it has been his whole life and I know he'd like to stay in the game, perhaps through goalkeeping coaching. Calum, our eldest son, wasn't really interested in football before the Newcastle game but the whole thing captured his imagination and now he would love to play. At the moment he is really into football stickers and I've asked him to look out for a picture of Alessandro Pistone. Calum says he'll try and do a swap for me. Then I'll keep it in my purse, usurping the current occupant, David Ginola . . .

Helen Saunders

Helen Saunders is married to Welsh international Dean. They both come from Swansea where Dean began his career before moving to clubs including Brighton, Oxford, Liverpool, Aston Villa and Galatasaray in Turkey.

I always seem to be having a baby when Dean gets a transfer. This time I was eight months pregnant with my little boy Callum when Dean came home to say the former Liverpool manager Graeme Souness was interested in signing him for the Turkish club he had just taken over. We'd often talked about Dean going to play abroad but I was thinking in terms of Spain or Portugal or Germany or France. I wasn't sure about Turkey. So anyway we decide to go for the weekend to take a look, even though I'm huge. We touch down in Istanbul and we're walking off the plane, it's boiling hot and Graeme's there saying 'Hello, how are you?' even though I don't know him that well. Suddenly what seems like thousands of Turkish men come running towards us. They pick Dean up and hoist him on their shoulders and carry him off. I'm left standing with our agent Kevin, who ushers me to the waiting car and I can see all these people carrying Dean towards us shouting, 'Saunders, Saunders' and I'm saying, 'Oh, Kevin, what's happening – he hasn't done anything yet!' 'I know,' he replies. 'It's mad.'

Dean is taken off in the morning and I'm left with Graeme's wife Karen. My ankles are like elephants' and I'm desperately tired. We eventually meet up on a boat for dinner. Dean is with the team and he's got the Galatasaray tracksuit on. 'What's going on?' I ask.

'I might be signing.'

'What do you mean?'

'Oh, it's a good deal – we can't afford to turn it down.'

'Why have you got all the kit on?'

'I'm going to the ground next.'

They'd arranged for Dean to be paraded around the Galatasaray ground. There were thousands of people in the stadium waiting to welcome him. So we came away and he had signed.

I met Dean in Swansea on Christmas Eve. I was 18 and working at the DVLC and all my friends used to finish work at lunchtime and go to the pub. Then we'd go on to a nightclub. They were all open in the afternoon on Christmas Eve. We ended up in Barons Club around three o'clock. There were only a few people scattered around, including Dean and his cousin standing at the bar. My cousin had a camera and said to the two lads, 'Come and have a photo with us.' So Dean came and stood next to me and we started chatting. I was quite merry and everything was a bit of a haze. At about six o'clock it was time to go home and change for the evening. Dean said, shall I see you later? Oh, OK. By the time we went back out the drink had worn off and I felt terrible so I sat in the pub with a glass of water in one hand and an umbrella in the other – it was pouring outside. Then I saw Dean and his cousin walk past the window and they were waving but they couldn't get in because the pub was so packed. I thought, oh that's a pity because he was ever so nice. Never mind.

But when I got to Barons he was there . . . It was getting late and I said I had to go and get a taxi. 'Don't worry,' Dean said. 'I've got the car.' I was taken aback. He was only 18 and yet he had a car. Also, on Christmas Eve people usually leave their cars at home so they can get drunk. But Dean had a injury – he had this big padding on his leg and he was limping – that's why he wasn't drinking. Outside my house he said, 'Can I see you tomorrow?'

'No, it's Christmas Day.'

'After dinner?'

'No.' I wasn't that keen.

'Where you going Boxing Day, then?'

'I've already got my tickets for the fancy-dress disco.'

'I'll be there.'

'OK. I'll see you.'

Dean didn't dress up but I went as a tennis player – complete with frilly knickers – and I won second place. From then on we saw each other every day, and every weekend we'd go down to the pier and play the slot machines. He was the first proper boyfriend I had.

After I met Dean I went home to my father who was a big Swansea supporter. As a child I'd been on the Vetchfield's north bank many a time, freezing, not really wanting to be there. But my father was an avid Swansea fan and used to take me and my brother down there all the time. My mother used to work in the evenings. She ran Tupperware parties and was, at one time, one of the top saleswomen in the country. So I said to my dad: 'This boy who I'm going out with says he plays football down the Vetch. His name's Dean Saunders.' 'I know him,' my dad said. It wasn't that I didn't believe Dean – I just didn't take it in. 'I know him – bring him home and we'll meet him.'

I don't know whether at the time my father was pleased because Dean played for Swansea or disgruntled because his daughter was going out with a footballer. He's very pleased now and both my mum and dad are exceptionally proud. Everyone's always thought the same as I did when I first met him: 'Nice boy, lovely boy, he is.'

I couldn't see myself leaving Swansea. I was quite happy – and then everything changed when Dean had to leave because the new manager John Bond didn't rate him. He was bought by Brighton & Hove Albion.

Brighton was like the ends of the earth to me. It was four hours away from Swansea. At this point we'd been going out together for three years and I was appalled that Dean didn't consider taking me. To me that meant, that's it then. But Dean said, no we see each other at the weekends. So he stayed in digs with a family. It was a difficult period and we ended up bickering, but eventually Dean managed to buy a house and I got a job at Gatwick airport and moved in with him. Within two weeks of starting my job Dean was transferred to Oxford. He played very well for them and scored lots of goals and the Oxford chairman, the infamous Robert Maxwell, told Dean: 'If you stick with me I'll make you a household name.' He was a big, larger-than-life character and although what he did to the *Mirror* pensioners was terrible, he was always fantastic to Dean.

The move to Oxford was my first taste of being left to do everything. Dean signed for the club and then he was gone. I put the house in Brighton up for sale and carried on with my job for a while but then Oxford were taking the players and their partners for a trip to Portugal for two weeks and I couldn't get time off work. So I packed in my job and moved up. We got married while Dean was at Oxford. It was January, so we only had a few days' honeymoon in London. The actress Catherine Zeta Jones came to my wedding because her parents were friends with Dean's mum and dad. She invited us to a show she was in – *42nd Street* in London's West End.

Danielle, our eldest daughter, was born in Oxford and we really enjoyed being there. Dean was earning more money and it was a very friendly place. But we'd just moved into a new house when we heard that Derby wanted to sign Dean. Derby County was also owned by the Maxwell family and the manager Arthur Cox came to see Dean. They went in one room with a bottle of whisky and I was in the other with the baby. I thought, 'what's going on?' Within a couple of hours Dean had signed.

But I know that the then Oxford manager, Mark Lawrenson, now a TV pundit, wasn't very happy that the deal had been done.

Derby was a lovely club, and we began a friendship with the player Mark Wright and his wife Sarah which was to stand us in good stead when Liverpool later came in to buy both Dean and Mark. I had just had my second little girl, Louisa. I was very happy at Derby and didn't really want to move but it was a huge step up for Dean. His father had played for Liverpool and of course Liverpool are one of the biggest clubs in the country. I was terrified about the move. I was really big after Louisa and I had no confidence. I was just petrified of the extra things that come with a glamorous club like Liverpool. One of the Liverpool players was Gary Ablett, and his wife Debbie was Mark Wright's cousin. She was giving Sarah a load of horror stories like having to wear a new designer outfit to every game otherwise you're looked down on.

A lot of players had been at Anfield a long time and there was a Liverpool way, but Graeme Souness had come along and put a bomb in the middle. He'd chucked several players out, done away with the old Boot Room and spent tons of money, so there was already a bit of upset in the club.

We lived in a hotel in the middle of Liverpool for three months with the two young children which was difficult, but Graeme being Graeme he didn't do things by halves. We had a suite and it was like a flat with two bedrooms, three bathrooms and a living room and dining room. We finally bought our dream house and Dean was doing really well scoring loads of goals and then we won the FA Cup against Sunderland in 1992. But despite all that, things weren't quite right at Liverpool.

It was also sometimes difficult when we went out. One night a group of us, players and their wives, went to the Continental in Liverpool, which is really a place for players rather than their wives. It was packed. We were standing upstairs looking over the balcony with the boys when suddenly this old bloke who worked there approached us. He had four young girls tottering behind him on their high heels wearing very skimpy outfits. He turned to them: 'There we are, girls. I told you all the footballers are in tonight. There we are. You can go and talk to them.' I thought, hold on a minute. I'm stood here – don't do that in front of me. So I went up to him and said, 'What are you doing?'

'I've brought the girls up to talk to the footballers.'

'Yes but we're here. We're stood here and I'm his wife and it's not very nice for me.'

'Oh go on with you,' said one of the girls and went up to Dean who was standing on the edge of the group.

'Hiya,' she smiled. 'Did you win today?'

'Is Jamie Redknapp here?' another one was asking.

'Did you score?' the first one continued and Dean gave me a what-can-I-do? look.

'Is Jamie Redknapp here?'

Ian Rush had been one of the longest-serving members of the Liverpool team and like Dean he is Welsh and I think it's been heart-breaking for both of them that Wales always seem to miss out on World Cup qualification. Dean has more than 60 caps and has scored 21 goals. As well as Rushy and Dean up front we've also had Mark Hughes and of course there's Ryan Giggs now. All that talent, yet the World Cup just passes us by every time. Once it was just down to a missed penalty.

We left Liverpool because Graeme Souness was told

by the board that he had to sell and it was a choice between Dean and Rushy, but we only found this out when we later joined up with Graeme in Turkey. Dean's last game for Liverpool was against Chelsea and it was in that game that Dean went in for a 50-50 tackle with Paul Elliott. Unfortunately it resulted in the Chelsea defender suffering a serious injury which subsequently forced him to retire. Dean then moved to Aston Villa, where we were astonished to be told that Paul Elliott was taking Dean to court for compensation. I thought, how could he do that? He was suing Liverpool and us personally for millions – we would have lost everything. It turned our lives upside down. I don't know what possessed him, except, of course, money.

The case hung over us for two years and really marred Dean's time at Aston Villa. But my best ever moment in Dean's career came during his first home game of the season for Villa. As so often happens in football they were drawn against Liverpool – the club where Dean felt he'd been forced out. So he did the best thing a striker can do – he scored two goals and Villa won. I was so thrilled and then this bloke came running down the steps in the stand and kissed me saying, 'Oh, love, I can't believe you're here. Fantastic. I'm glad you came to this club.'

There was such a different atmosphere at Aston Villa. It was, I think, the best club we've been to. The wives were lovely and there was a crèche too. At the end of the season the players were due to fly out to Mauritius where they were taking part in an exhibition game against Everton. The Goodison players weren't allowed to take their wives but the Villa manager Ron Atkinson and his wife Maggie made sure all the Villa wives and girlfriends had an all-expenses-paid trip, staying in the best hotel on the island.

Although over the two years Dean was always having

to go to meetings with Liverpool officials or his solicitors regarding the court action started by Paul Elliott, I only realised just how much it was preying on his mind when after an Aston Villa Coca-Cola Cup win where everyone was having a great time celebrating, Dean just couldn't enjoy himself. He really wasn't very happy at all. We ended up having a row because he was so fed up. So I was glad when at last the court case was heard in London. It lasted two weeks and the judge found in Dean's favour. A terrible strain had been lifted from our lives.

But then Ron Atkinson was sacked from Villa and Brian Little came in as manager. It was a very unsettling time and that's when Graeme Souness stepped in to take Dean to Turkey. Mike Marsh and Barry Venison who had been at Liverpool with Dean had also signed but they didn't stay very long. In all we were out there for a season. We rented a villa overlooking the Bosphorus, where all the very rich live, and had a lot of our own stuff shipped over.

I also had Callum there. If he had been my first baby I would have come home but he was my third so I told the hospital I would be fine as long as they had some gas and air. Luckily my mother was there when the baby started and they rushed me down to the labour suite. When we got there the doctor said, 'Do you want it the Turkish way or the English way?' Apparently most Turkish women have epidurals and they didn't have any gas and air so Callum was born at 4 a.m. without any pain relief.

By the morning there were about 30 pressmen outside the door and they wanted me on the TV. Dean said, 'You're going to have to let them in or they won't go away.' It was a small room and around midday a procession of them, about ten at a time, would come in with the TV crews and film us and take photos. They were very happy and thrilled: 'Please hold the baby.' 'What's his name?' When I told them Callum, they all fell about laughing. 'You can't call him that,' they said. 'It means pencil in Turkish.' I had to laugh but I couldn't wait for them all to just go away.

The press and TV interest was the same wherever we went. If we went out for a meal the restaurant owner would phone the papers and within ten minutes there'd be a photographer there. It was a huge goldfish bowl: 'Saunders, Saunders,' the fans would chant. They are so fanatical that they have been known to shoot themselves if the national team loses.

Galatasaray won the Cup when we were there but we couldn't go for a night out after the game. We were stuck in the flat of Brad Friedel – now the Liverpool goalkeeper – because the fans had jammed the streets with their cars, waving flags and beeping their horns. If we had tried to go out they would have mobbed us. It was mad, absolutely mad and quite frightening. Of course we were treated like kings and queens when Dean was winning but if you lose they don't speak to you – they take it all very personally.

What was also worrying for us was that Louisa was very ill with asthma while we were there. It was brought on by the air pollution, which was terrible. We were always in and out of hospital with her. One time Dean was away for three days and Louisa was coughing and spluttering and catching her breath. I had to ask Karen, Graeme's wife, to look after Danielle and Callum while I drove Louisa to the hospital. But getting in your car was frightening in itself. It's like *Wacky Races* out there. Every time you get in the car you think you're going to get bumped. Graeme Souness had only signed a one-year contract so we decided to come home and Frank Clark then came in for Dean at Nottingham Forest.

We'd been in our new house three months when Dave Bassett took over as manager at Forest and decided he didn't want Dean. Oh no, I thought. I couldn't bear to move again. Luckily Sheffield United came in. Then Nigel Spackman, the manager, left and they got knocked out in the first division play-offs. Now everything is changing at Sheffield. I haven't felt settled since we left Aston Villa and I must admit I'm on edge and a little bit frightened about what will happen next . . .

Viv Neate

Viv Neate has been washing the Reading FC first-team kit for more than 20 years. She is married to head groundsman Gordon, who played for the club in the 1960s.

I don't know what the neighbours used to think when they got a glimpse of me in the early hours of the morning in my dressing gown taking in black bags from a strange man. It happened quite often – well, after every Reading away match because Ron, the football club's kit man, would drop off the dirty shirts, shorts and socks at whatever time the first team arrived back in Reading after a game. My kit washing started when my husband Gordon had to finish his career as a footballer in the 60s because of a knee injury. He was offered the Reading groundsman's job and later I was asked to look after the kit as the laundry wasn't making a very good job of it. It was something I could do while the children were at home so I said I'd give it a go. More than twenty years later I'm still doing it.

When I first started I wanted to make a good impression and I'd give the shorts a good spray of starch – that didn't last very long but I always told the players: play well you'll get Comfort in your socks; play badly, no Comfort. My neighbour was very good, taking a bit of her fence down so I could use her washing line as well and I must admit when I hung the kit out I used to worry that something might get pinched, but it never did. Of course the children in the house on the other side loved it and often brought their friends round. They'd ask, 'Can I touch the number 9 shirt?' or whoever the hero was that day. One thing that I've always thought is a little peculiar is washing the players' slips as well. I mean, it's a very personal thing and when Gordon was playing he had his own jockstrap which I used to wash for him. I did ask the players once if they wouldn't rather take their slips away to wash themselves. But they were quite happy for me to wash them and then to get any old slip back. It was clean, of course, but it had certainly been worn by someone else the week before . . .

Gordon and I both shed a tear when Reading played their last home game at the old Elm Park ground at the end of the 1997–98 season. Gordon had been grounds-man there for 32 years and he knew every blade of grass. I stopped washing the kit at home that season. Reading's new Madejski stadium has its own laundry facilities built in, but I'll never forget all those shirts on the line in my back garden or the strange request I had from a fanatical fan, David Downs. David is a retired teacher and the club historian and has been involved with the Reading Primary School team for years. In 1988 Reading reached the Simod Cup Final and the club went to Wembley for the first time. David didn't want an ordinary keepsake like a programme or a commemorative plate. No, he wanted the water the players' shirts had been washed in after the match. I nearly flooded my kitchen stopping the washing machine halfway through the non-fast coloureds cycle. But I got David his bottle of dirty water, which to this day has pride of place among his Reading FC memorabilia.

It was a wonderful day going to Wembley for the Simod Cup but my best day out there was when Reading reached the first division play-off finals several seasons ago. We were treated like VIPs and had a fantastic time. It's still amazing how close Reading were to going into the Premiership – they were 2–0 up on Bolton at one stage but then they missed a penalty and finally lost the game.

Gordon and I first met at the Co-op social club in the early 60s. I was working in the baby department at the Co-op and my friend Doreen and I often went to the social after work. It was near Reading Football Club in the west end of town but I lived on the other side in an area called Whitley. My district was infamous for the Whitley Whiff, a peculiar smell which came from the huge rubbish tip nearby. Reading's new stadium is built virtually on top of that tip . . .

Doreen and I went to the Co-op social for the dancing and we had our eye on a group of lads who came to play snooker and pool. Gordon was a part of this group and when he asked me out I said yes, but I wasn't that bothered. In fact I was only doing it because my friend quite liked the look of him. Well, we hit it off but I didn't know this gang of lads were footballers. My family weren't interested in football – I didn't even know where Elm Park was. Gordon was in Reading reserves at the time but he didn't tell me. I only found out when one of the guys downstairs at the Co-op asked me if I was going out with Fred. 'Who?' I said, not knowing that this was Gordon's nickname. 'Fred, who plays in the Reading stiffs,' came the reply. He got his nickname from Fred Carney's circus as he was always the joker.

After I met Gordon the dancing stopped because he had two left feet, but one of the perks of being a footballer was that you got free passes to the pictures and we often used to watch a film and then have some dinner at a place across the road. When Gordon got into the first team I went to watch him. The first-team crowds then were huge even at Reading, who were at the time in the old third division south. But I sometimes found it rather boring, so I'd go over to his mum's for a cup of tea instead.

After we got married I moved into the block of flats owned by the club. All the players lived there. It was a good idea because it meant while the men were away playing football you had all the wives around so you weren't left on your own. It also made for good team spirit. But back then things were much more financially precarious. In the summer the players' wages were cut in half so Gordon and the former Reading manager Maurice Evans got jobs painting and decorating for Wokingham District Council. Most players were only on one-year contracts so at the end of the season there was a terrible wait for the registered letter which told you whether you'd been retained or not.

I worked at a shoe shop called Milwards and Gordon would meet me in town at lunchtime after his two-hour training and we'd go and eat at the Cadena. Then he'd go home and muggins here had to go back to work. Something's wrong here, I thought. So I gave up work. Then Gordon suffered a bad injury playing away at Walsall. He had damaged his cruciate ligament and was in hospital for a month. I'd just had my second baby and we didn't have a car so I'd struggle up to the hospital on the bus every day. It was a terrible time but gradually Gordon recovered, only to suffer a cartilage problem. At 25 years old he was finished as a professional footballer. Roy Bentley, the former England and Chelsea player, was Reading manager at the time and he suggested Gordon should take over the vacant groundsman job. He jumped at the chance. It meant he was still in football, still involved with the players, still with his beloved Reading. And he's still there now tending the new pitch at the Madejski stadium after all these years and all the changes of management and players. I think that's why everyone wants to talk to him. People have come and gone but Gordon goes on. Even if we're on holiday someone will spot him, and if we go shopping I know it'll be me doing all the work while he's chatting away to a fan . . .

Kirsty Dailly

Kirsty is married to Scottish international Christian Dailly who began his career at Dundee United and is now with Derby County in the Premiership. Christian played for Scotland in the recent World Cup finals in France.

We were all singing 'Flower of Scotland' in the buffet car as the train pulled into Gare de Montparnasse in Paris. I had one of Christian's Scotland shirts tied around my waist but it was still hard to take in. My husband was playing for Scotland in the opening match of the World Cup and against the current world champions, Brazil.

My family and a group of friends – 20 of us and six kids – were staying in *gîtes* near Bordeaux but now we were off to the Stade de France surrounded by the Tartan Army. Men in kilts, women carrying flags, kids with the Scottish flag painted on their faces. Most were singing and everyone was so optimistic. It was a very special feeling to be part of it all and you felt proud to be Scottish in Paris that day.

Me and my stepdad Stuart – naturally in a kilt – travelled on the Métro to meet up with Christian's family in the stadium. My sister Sally and four of our friends didn't manage to get tickets so they headed off to the Eiffel Tower to watch the game on a giant screen. The stadium was magnificent. Brazilians and Scots sang and partied together – dozens of Scots were even wearing Brazil tops with their kilts. I hadn't eaten a thing all day – I just couldn't. I don't think I've ever felt this nervous about a football match before.

The opening ceremony seemed to last about eight hours but I didn't dare move from my seat just in case I wasn't able to get back in time and missed the kick-off. Of course it was disappointing to lose to Brazil, particularly after we'd equalised, but the way Scotland played gave us real hope for the following two group matches against

Norway and Morocco. After the match we were escorted to a reception room to meet up with the team. I was so proud of Christian for being part of the game, part of what the Tartan Army had been shouting and singing about. We walked together out through the players' tunnel on to the pitch. It was absolutely amazing and more than a little scary even now when the stadium was empty. Christian said he had just tried to soak it all up and enjoy it but it couldn't have been easy – there had been 80,000 supporters watching in the stadium and another billion people on TV all around the world.

It was hard to say goodbye as the team left and I did feel a bit lonely as I went to meet my sister, but more than anything I felt pride, and I wanted to shout out that I was married to Christian Dailly. I didn't need to when my sister was there because she made sure everyone knew. The fans wanted to shake my hand or hug and kiss me. Sometimes they wouldn't believe her and they just stared at me, probably trying to decide whether or not a woman wearing a Scotland shirt four sizes too big with a saltire painted on her arm could possibly be a footballer's wife – weren't they supposed to be glamorous?

On the day Scotland played Norway in Bordeaux, I gave my ticket to my mum and flew south with my two young daughters Rosie and Christy to Marseilles. I wanted to be at the team's base camp as soon as the period we were able to be with the players began the following day. So the three of us watched the match in our hotel room. We all went mad when Craig Burley equalised and Scotland were so unlucky not to go on and win. Christian had a great game. I'm not usually a very good judge of how he has played but I could tell easily this time.

There were five days until the next game so I drove up to Orleans, where I had studied for a year, to visit the family I had au-paired for. While we were there a journalist from the *Daily Record* in Glasgow phoned to interview me about being a player's wife in the World Cup – the third such interview and the same question: What's it like to be a football widow? Well, here I was with my friends having a fantastic time watching my husband represent his country – why should I feel sorry for myself?

I took the children to the last game against Morocco, in Saint Etienne. I was worried that with the kick-off at nine o'clock they would be tired and grumpy but they were brilliant. Although Scotland were put out of the World Cup that night it was still a great place to be. The supporters stood in the stadium and sang for ages after the match despite the fact that we'd lost 3–0.

Of course we were all gutted. I had already bought tickets for the next game in case Scotland got through. As it was, even if they had won against Morocco it would have been in vain as Norway had beaten Brazil for a second group place behind the world champions. It was a strange feeling knowing that the World Cup would carry on without Scotland, and it didn't seem fair.

Christian had been involved in international football at under-21 level since he was 16 years old. This was when the tabloids began to label him the 'Peter Pan of football'. Now he had come home from France with his thirteenth senior cap – and some smelly mementoes. I've never minded washing any of Christian's kit – his socks and so on. But he'd stuffed his Scotland shirts and those he had swapped in the World Cup in the bottom of his kitbag. After he'd been home a week I plucked up the courage to open it, although I took Christian's advice and unzipped the bag outside. Hadji, Morocco's star striker, had exchanged shirts as had a Norwegian player. There they were: a crumpled, damp, sweaty, pongy heap. He didn't manage to get a Brazilian shirt but there's always the World Cup in 2002.

Christian and I met at school. He was a year older than me and in my brother's class. You know what it's like in the playground and Christian was one of those really popular guys – he was the centre of attention, always laughing and having a good time. He'd be playing football in the playground and he was always one of the best. The girls all used to watch out for him in the corridors; 'Oh, look, there's Christian Dailly.' We went out when I was 14. Christian was my first ever boyfriend but I chucked him after six weeks. I can't remember why exactly.

Christian left school at 16 and soon began playing in Dundee United's first team but he appeared at the school one day and walked me home. He then phoned and we went out again. I got a bit of stick from my friends who said, you're only going out with him because he's a footballer. But it wasn't that at all. I hadn't seen him for a long time and you know when you're with somebody and you feel comfortable and since then, since I was 15, we've always been together.

I left school at 17 and this was when I went to France to study French, geography and literature. Christian and I missed each other horrendously but the experience was well worth the year apart. I still have a big box of letters that he sent. He was very good. I received at least one a week but of course his box of letters from me is bigger – I think I started off writing eight a week. While I was there I applied to do a hotel and catering management degree and took up an offer from Edinburgh University. So Christian and I had another year apart, although I became pregnant with Rosie so that was the end of my degree.

By the time Rosie was due Dundee United were in the middle of the build-up for their Coca-Cola Cup semi-final match against Celtic. She eventually arrived on Monday morning and Christian phoned in to the club to say he was missing training that day to be at the birth. As the semi-final wasn't until the Wednesday night he didn't think there would be a problem and rang the club to say he'd meet them in Glasgow. But no, this wasn't good enough and the message from the manager Ivan Golac, was: 'Stay there, Christian, just don't bother coming. You're not in the squad – you're dropped.'

Apparently he'd got his priorities all wrong wanting to be with me at the birth of his first child. Heaven forbid. The press had a field day. We were bombarded at the hospital by phone calls. A TV crew was waiting on the doorstep when Christian got home. We were under siege and all I kept thinking was, this is strange. What's the interest? I've just had a baby. I was only 19 and I wasn't used to press attention. It was scary and unwelcome. They wanted photographs but nobody looks their best when they've just had a baby so there was no chance of that. But of course they didn't want a nice photograph so they could say congratulations to Kirsty and Christian on the birth of your first daughter. They wanted it to show the reason why Golac dropped Dailly. Footballers have got to get used to press attention but this wasn't fair, and it wasn't fair of the manager. He knew exactly what he was doing. He used the papers over the next couple of days to say he had been misunderstood. Apparently he hadn't dropped Christian because he missed training but because he would not be in the right frame of mind. Sure.

By contrast, at Derby County, when our second daughter Christy was born the day before Derby played Arsenal, Christian also missed training but still played the next day and in fact won the Man of the Match award.

I think our treatment at Dundee United may have had something to do with the fact that Christian had been there such a long time. Thirteen years. He'd played for them since he was a little boy and the footballing education he received there was second to none but until we left he was still seen as a boy.

Of course there were some good times at Dundee United and the highlight was winning the Scottish FA Cup in 1994. We were playing Rangers, the champions, so it was very glamorous and Dundee United were the real underdogs – we'd been to the Cup Final before but never won. It was so exciting watching Christian walk out with the team and then wave up at me. He set up the winning goal when his shot hit the post and Craig Brewster knocked it in – a great day.

When Christian's contract was up at Dundee United, they wanted him to sign another and the club told us that no one else was interested. Well, how did we know that this was true? So although we had always been wary of agents we decided to get one. Our new agent said that the Bosman ruling meant Christian could move abroad for free without a transfer fee being paid, and that the Spanish club Celta Vigo were interested. So we went out to Spain and were treated like royalty by Celta Vigo.

While we were considering their offer, Manchester City declared an interest so we went to meet Francis Lee, the City chairman, and Alan Ball, the manager. They brought their wives along and we went for a Chinese meal. I thought, wow what is going on – this is scary, this is amazing. Christian would have been happy to sign for Manchester City but Francis Lee wouldn't meet Dundee United's transfer fee demands because of course within Britain the Bosman ruling didn't apply, so the deal fell through.

We were stuck in the middle thinking, oh my God

we've got to go to Spain, and then all of a sudden Derby County came up. Christian met Jim Smith, the manager. He went down with his dad and signed two days later.

If Christian were ever to leave Derby we wouldn't use an agent again. In fact we decided not to use him when Christian signed for Derby – although we still had to pay him because of contractual obligations. Agents are businessmen and as such are out for what *they* want. They tell you that everything they are doing for you is in your best interest as a footballer but they want to earn money too and they are ruthless.

All footballers should have a good financial adviser because the money they earn in so short a career has to be invested wisely for the future. Earning a lot of money early on can be deceptive security-wise, particularly if a footballer starts living a high lifestyle, only to find that his career is over and he hasn't saved anything. We save as much as we can. We don't need to have a mansion. Some players feel they do – they buy these huge houses with swimming pools – but if we did that, when Christian stopped playing it would be hard to move down again.

Christian has had his fair share of injuries and while he was at Dundee United he had several cartilage operations on his knee, but subsequent keyhole surgery has cured the problem and he hasn't had any trouble since. Christian says it's because he takes cod-liver oil. He has a cupboard full of vitamins that he swears by. He'll have the odd glass of wine but he'll never drink before a game. But no amount of vitamins can save you from a kick in the head. I was watching the match live on the television when Derby were playing Bolton, and saw Christian go in to head the ball when the opposing player came in with a high kick. Oh no, I thought. He's had his teeth smashed in. In fact his jaw was broken and the other player didn't even get a booking or a free kick against him, although the referee apologised to Christian later because he didn't see it. His chin was actually loose from his face because his jaw had broken on either side of it. It was horrible. He had to travel back from Bolton and I met him in the Accident and Emergency department in Derby Royal Infirmary where he had an X-ray. You should have seen Christian's face – he looked like Desperate Dan. The X-rays showed a couple of fractures but fortunately one of the best surgeons in this field was working in Derby and he did a wonderful job.

When Christian finshes in football he would like to be a rock star – not a pop star, a rock star. He loves music, particularly the Stone Roses – Ian Brown and John Squire are both heroes of his. He also likes the Seahorses, John Squire's new band, and the Beatles. He plays the guitar and has written a song and his ambition is to be in a band. I suppose being in the video of Del Amitri's World Cup song *Don't Come Home Too Soon* is a step in the right direction . . .

David was Welsh. His father had worked down the mines in Wales before the war and then he brought his family to Northampton where he ran a youth club. I used to go down there every night after school and the girls would have activities such as cookery lessons on one side of the hall and the boys would be on the other side doing things like woodwork. Then at nine o'clock we would meet in the middle and have music and dancing until ten. That's how I met David; and Des O'Conner, he was a member too. There were boxing tournaments and I used to take a PE class. I was always keen on athletics and I think if women had been playing football in my time I would have had a go – I loved all sports. It really was an idyllic time.

David and I decided to get married on my 21st birthday but I had to have a back operation. They wheeled my birthday cake into the hospital ward, I blew out the candles and then went straight to the operating theatre. We finally got married a year later and then everything changed because in 1950 David was transferred from Northampton Town to Arsenal. David had played rugby in Wales but when his family came to England he won a schoolboy cap for football and began to play for Northampton Town. He went to do his National Service and was spotted by Arsenal when Pat Whittaker, the son of the Arsenal manager Tom, was on the same camp and recommended David to his father.

I was very nervous about leaving Northampton and going to London but Arsenal did everything possible to make it easier for us. I remember seeing the marble halls at Highbury for the first time, with the bust of Herbert Chapman looking benevolently down on you. It was wonderful, so glamorous. We lived in Cockfosters in one of the club houses. Tommy Docherty lived around the corner and Jimmy Bloomfield lived opposite. David had to wait for his chance to play in the first team as the left half position was taken by the great Joe Mercer but we couldn't fail to be impressed by Arsenal from the beginning and we were happy to wait.

Footballers were real heroes – even then. There were huge crowds and wherever we went supporters would want David's autograph. It was still the same long after he retired. We would go down to the golf club and people would approach us. 'Hello, Mrs Bowen,' they would say and then it was straight on to David and the football. Football was the all-consuming factor in our lives together. During the festive season, for example, David would play a match on Christmas Day and on Boxing Day and if a Saturday fell just before, it would be three days in a row.

A footballer's wages by the standards of the day were quite good, with David earning £15 during the season and £12 in the summer. Before the maximum wage structure was broken by Jimmy Hill's challenge everyone was paid the same so there was never any animosity, but I can recall being told that the musicians playing in the band at half-time at Highbury were being paid more than the team. Arsenal must have made a lot of money with those huge crowds, and not a great deal of it went to the players.

David finally got his chance to play in the first team when dear Joe Mercer broke his leg. He subsequently went on to be made captain, which was a great honour. There were some wonderful matches at Highbury but one occasion was particularly poignant. It was Arsenal against Manchester United on a Saturday in February 1958, just before Matt Busby's team went off to play in Belgrade. Manchester United won 5–4 but five of the team playing on that day were to die in the Munich air disaster on their return home from Europe just five days later. David knew all the Busby Babes and he was terribly upset when the news came in.

But there were happier times and none more so than when we learned David had won his first Welsh cap on the day our daughter Lynn was born. David's family were delighted he was playing for his country and Wales then had an excellent side which David went on to captain. I have a wonderful photograph, taken just before an Anglo-Welsh international, of him leading out Wales and Billy Wright leading out the England team.

David was an inspirational captain and it was during the 1958 World Cup that he led Wales to their greatest ever footballing triumph when they reached the quarter-finals and were drawn against Brazil. Pele was 17 at the time and it was his first World Cup. Of course we had no television so we had to content ourselves with following the game on the radio – even the players had to wait until they got home to see their World Cup heroics at the cinema on the Pathé News. There were no goals in the first half as the Welsh defence managed to keep the Brazilians at bay. But Wales were missing the great John Charles through injury and after 66 minutes Pele's shot was deflected past our goalkeeper Jack Kelsey – the only goal of the game and the one that Pele has often described as the most important he ever scored. David came home from Sweden with a beautiful commemorative glass vase. I love flowers in the house so it was the perfect memento.

Once his playing days for Arsenal were over, David returned to Northampton Town to finish his career as player-manager. At the time we shared the ground with the cricket club and as the beginning of the football season overlapped with the end of the cricket one the first few games of the season were always played away. Consequently we usually had a sticky start to the season.

David increased his workload when, once he had stopped playing, he also took on the management of the Welsh side on a part-time basis. It entailed him training the team in Northampton in the morning and then travelling down to Cardiff or wherever to watch a match on the national side's behalf in the evening. Then there was the Northampton scouting to do – the club didn't have any staff so David did it himself. I often went with him to keep him company and catch up on conversation. Even now I know a town from its floodlights.

David always said creating a team was like making a cake. You've got to get the mix right, the balance, and I think that's what's wrong with Wales today. There are brilliant, individual players but they just can't play together. David was hampered in his management of the national side by something which is still a problem today – club managers failing to release their players for international duty. I know it frustrated him greatly. But there were bonuses in being the Wales manager and one of them was that David could attract good Welsh players to Northampton and the club achieved the remarkable feat of being promoted from the fourth to the first division in just five seasons from 1960 to 1965.

The town put on a civic reception but David was out scouting and so he arrived late. That was typical. He worked so hard and achieved so much but even when we reached the first division there was still no money forthcoming for players and we were relegated after only one season. It was soul-destroying. There was a huge difference between the divisions and however hard we worked, Northampton were always the poor relation. I recall the journalist Ken Jones coming to interview David at the old County Ground and saying that he was sure David was two inches taller from all the dust that came through the ceiling of his manager's office.

After Lynn – the daughter who once swapped a football card with a picture of her father on it for a marble – we had two sons and the inevitable question was: would they be footballers? David didn't encourage Keith and Barry. He was adamant that academic work came first. But they did both play in between their studying. In fact Keith, who played for teams including Northampton, Brentford and Colchester, worked as an accountant in the day and then trained on his own in the park in the evenings. David would often come across fathers who were living their lives through their up-and-coming young footballing sons. He would try to get them to realise that only a few made the grade and that it was important to enjoy it – to smell the roses.

I have a picture of all my grandchildren in Arsenal shirts. David loved that club and to play for them was the best part of his career. I have donated one of David's football shorts to the Highbury museum and one day when my grandchildren are old enough we will all go down to the Arsenal and then they will really understand just how special David was.

Kelly Woan

Kelly is married to Ian Woan who began his career with non-league Runcorn and now plays for Nottingham Forest FC. She is from Seattle and met Ian when he was on holiday with Teddy Sheringham in Hawaii. She is studying part-time for a master's degree in psychology.

I first saw Ian on a catamaran off Waikiki beach. I had flown from Seattle to Hawaii to join up with three friends on a six-day break. On the second night we were invited to a party on the catamaran. An hour and a half into the trip my friend noticed these guys. We went over to talk to them and we thought, oh they're Australian. Wow, say something: 'G'day, mate.' They were really offended – all three of them, but I noticed Ian was sort of retiring, hanging back in the corner. I also noticed how attractive he was and, I suppose you could say, our eyes met. He was very shy and left most of the talking to the other two, who turned out to be Teddy Sheringham and Keith Stevens, the Millwall player.

A big reason why I was most attracted to Ian in the first place was that he was not in a pair of Speedos. Most American girls hate guys that wear Speedos – they're so unattractive. Ian was the only one who had a proper pair of American swim-trunks on so we were kind of laughing at the guys who were wearing Speedos. The only guys in Hawaii who wore Speedos were the body builders and the strippers – but Teddy and Keith were not body-building material.

My friend Sheila was also impressed by Ian. Hey, I was 21, I was on holiday and I thought, well if you like him you can have him and I'll find someone else – but really inside I was thinking, I really like this guy. OK, I'd just met him, I didn't know anything about him, but I liked him. I liked his accent – I'm a sucker for an English accent – most American girls are. When we docked on the beach, we arranged to meet up at a reggae bar later that night for a drink and, in fact, although collectively we were all having a laugh, Ian and I weren't really hitting it off that well. I liked him, but I was pretending that I didn't. He wasn't saying very much and what he did say was very sarcastic. But then he asked me to dance, and I only realised later how special this was – because Ian doesn't dance. So we danced to the last song and he said, 'If you lived around the corner I'd ask you to marry me tomorrow.' I laughed it off, but inside I thought, 'and I'd say yes.'

We spent the last five days of my holiday together, and when he left me at the airport I remember feeling a great loss. I was crying my eyes out and just wishing Ian lived in Seattle. He was a bit emotional too. So, although I don't think of myself as the type to pursue anyone, I must admit I did. I sent him a dozen red roses; long-stemmed red roses – it was probably the first time he'd ever been sent flowers. And we kept in touch: letters, phone calls and I had loads of pictures to remind me of him.

On that night when we first met we sat on the beach after our dance in the bar and I asked Ian what he did for a living. When he said he was a footballer I thought, what's that? Because we just wouldn't call it that. Then I just started laughing and he said, 'What's so funny?'

'You can't be a footballer.'

'Why not?' he said.

'You're too small,' I replied, visualising this six-foot-four, 300-pound ball player.

'No, no, not American football. Soccer, I play soccer.'

That made sense. I had a few boyfriends back home who played soccer, but they all had regular jobs because you can't make a living out of playing soccer in the States. So I suppose I just thought Ian had a normal day job. I didn't realise how big football is in England until I came here. In America soccer is considered to be a real nicey, nicey game and is played by the guys who can't make the football or the baseball team. They tend to be the smaller, shorter, weedier ones.

So they laughed, everybody in my family laughed, when I told them Ian played soccer for a living. My dad said soccer was for wimps. Ian was really offended and tried to explain that soccer had an entirely different culture in England. Prior to the World Cup in 1994 my family didn't realise how important it is as a global game. They didn't even understand the rules. My grandfather was delighted though because he had played soccer in England before he emigrated – and in the same position as Ian. So it wasn't until one of my relatives saw Ian playing on ESPN, the sports cable network, that we all thought 'wow'.

Seven months passed before my friend and I finally went over to England for a holiday. It was just before Christmas in 1992. Ian was with the Forest team preparing for a match against Tottenham Hotspur so his friends picked us up from the airport. We laughed at silly things like the toilets flushing a different way and not being able to plug in our hair-dryers, but we got a real shock when we got to White Hart Lane. We just couldn't believe that that many people would go to watch a soccer match. Back home there would be maybe two or three thousand people – here we were part of a 30,000-plus crowd. We sat in the away end and couldn't understand what everyone was screaming about. And then when I saw Ian run out on to the field – and remember, I hadn't seen him in seven months – I just couldn't believe that all these people were there to watch him. It was awe-inspiring.

We had planned to spend the evening in London but Forest lost and the coach made all the players, including Ian, go back on the bus to Nottingham. So we stayed down and went out with Teddy Sheringham and some of his friends and that was amazing too: the players were treated like Hollywood stars, people wanting their autographs, staring and so on. But we knew them, we'd even seen them in their Speedos, so we thought, why do you want their autographs?

That summer Ian came over to Seattle and I was determined to finish it because of the distance between us, the huge phone bills and all the uncertainty. But when Ian arrived all the emotions came flooding back and he asked me to move to England with him. It was a big decision. My mom tried to stop me. 'Why couldn't you have met a nice American boy?' But my dad said, 'If it makes you happy.' Then the day before I was due to leave I thought, what am I doing? I don't even know this guy; I've probably spent a total of 20 days with him. But I'd booked a 45-day stay ticket and I thought after that I'd know one way or the other. Well, I'm still here.

I married Ian because I love him desperately but I think if I hadn't loved sport, and football in particular, and enjoyed going to the games, I would have found it very difficult to marry him and stay. Most players are fans of football anyway and it doesn't stop when they come home from training or the match on the Saturday. It's watching every game on TV, which with satellite is virtually every night, and then talking about it. It's just something you have to accept.

On a match day Ian is always very nervous, so I've learned, over the years, to leave him to himself. He's very quiet. He does a lot of pacing about and has a ritual. The evening before, pasta and lots of water and then in the morning, breakfast, watching TV on the couch until it's time to go. If he can't follow this routine for some reason he gets quite anxious. He's not really superstitious, it's just that food, rest and water are the best preparation. But when he has lost his form he scrutinises his routine and often changes something, even if it's something really tiny, to try and get it back.

Footballers are so obsessed with the art of peaking at just the right time for the match that sometimes there's not an awful lot of time for them to think about sex. When Ian first told me that there was a no sex rule the night before a game I couldn't believe it. Then I heard the other players talking about it so I knew it was true. It's really the last thing on a player's mind. If they've spent time carefully preparing they don't want to do anything that might waste energy! But actually I think it's more of a mental thing – the night before a match their mind's on other things. I understand that: the pressure on professional footballers is really quite terrifying. I remember when Ian injured his knee and was out for three months. Those were awful days, with both of us worried that he would never recover properly or that he wouldn't get back into the first team. He was so depressed and isolated himself from the fit players. All the injured players do the same thing. They seem to feel they're not part of the team any more. Ian comes home after nearly every match battered and bruised. It really scares me. He played two games in one week when he had nine stitches in his head and eye. Fans don't realise the wear and tear on the players' bodies. Lots of players still play when they're injured because of the pressure on team places. The fact is they want to be part of the team and that means more to them than anything else.

A few months after I came to live in England Ian picked up an injury and it was around the time of the Christmas do at Forest. Frank Clark was manager – Brian Clough was only there for a short while with Ian, and from what I can make out Ian was petrified of him. Anyway, Ian was trying to fight his way back into the team. He's always been the club joker, always one of the first with the banter in the dressing room, so I think the management thought he could cope with losing his place, that it wouldn't get him down. I hadn't met Frank Clark before and Ian was joking at the dinner table saying 'Go and talk to the manager and ask him why I'm not in the team.' So a bit later on he introduced me to Frank. I could see the whole table sniggering and thinking, oh no, what's she going to say. We started talking and eventually I came out with it and asked why Ian wasn't in the team and then gave him all the reasons why I thought he should be. It can't have done any harm because the next game Ian was back in the team.

Forest had a terrible 96–97 season, being relegated after finishing bottom of the Premiership and Ian felt that really badly too. He used to say that the adverse comments in the newspapers and the abuse from the fans didn't bother him, but it does. Every footballer would be lying to you if they said it didn't affect them. Yes, there are pressures in all jobs, but to play in front of 30–40,000 fans who are screaming at you, and a lot of them don't like you and are calling you names – it's difficult. It does get to you and I feel I want to be there for him. But Ian, like a lot of British guys, likes to keep things bottled up. He is getting better but I still find that we often have to have a silly argument about something not being cooked right before it all comes out. It did get to the stage where I used to dread him coming through the door, thinking, oh no, what sort of mood is he going to be in today?

I find it particularly difficult to cope when the fans get on to him during the match. If Ian is playing terribly then I will be the first to say so. But it makes me mad when people say 'No wonder they don't care when they are being paid so much money.' In fact, one Forest fan suggested they should have their wages taken away, then they might play better. That's rubbish. The money is not the reason why they are out there and there is no way he goes out there to play badly. Sometimes when I sit in the stands, in amongst the fans, some of them get off on the fact that they recognise me and start shouting gratuitous insults about Ian. I'm not one of those meddling wives, but I'm not going to sit there and put up with being verbally abused so I give as good as I get. But if I say something they just laugh and say, 'I've paid my money, I can say what I like.'

Some of the fan mail is really funny – pictures of young women in their lingerie with their telephone numbers on the back. Well, I suppose it's a laugh now that I'm used to it. Ian always answers the letters from children. He was a Liverpool fan as a boy, so he knows how they feel. But we also get letters from Africa asking for bikes or 16 pairs of football boots for the team. The strangest request was from a guy who wanted to come and live with us, I suppose in a sort of housekeeping capacity. Come to think of it, maybe I should have taken him up on the offer.

We've had our problems with the lot at the other end as well – I mean with the previous regime at Forest where it seemed to me the board and the players never saw eye to eye on anything. There was definitely a feeling that we were second-class citizens. For years we didn't have a players' lounge. Then we had a tiny room, hardly big enough for all the children of the players let alone their guests. Of course the directors had their own bar. When Forest were playing in Europe in the UEFA Cup we had to pay for our own transport and tickets. In Auxerre we sat with the Forest fans, which was fine except that there was a terrible crush and the crowd was getting tear-gassed. The players were really worried about us and Stuart Pearce, the club captain, went to the board and demanded that the next game we should sit with the other executives. This was granted, although we still had to pay.

The club treats the players like little boys. And I've always thought that if you are treated like a little boy, you are going to act like one. The players are given very little sense of responsibility. The club does everything for them. They are told what to eat, what time to go to bed, what time to get up, report for training. It's like a mother telling her children what to do and the amazing thing is, they do it. Some of them never grow up. They don't know how to adjust to responsibility or commitment. Since a lot of these guys were 16 they've had people telling them that they're great and that they can do no wrong, so it's inevitable that some of the guys start believing it. One thing that I am grateful for is that Ian came into the game at 22 from a non-league club – Runcorn. He would have been a quantity surveyor if he hadn't been a footballer. So he knows what it is like to work from nine to five and have some responsibility. He's more down to earth than some of the players are, and I'm grateful for that. It also means he has other interests outside football, including golf, which we play together.

I definitely feel the pressure of being the wife of somebody famous. It took me a long time to get used to it. When I met Ian I had absolutely no idea he was some sort of 'catch'. And I hate it when he introduces me to someone and they completely ignore me. They're not interested in me: as far as they're concerned I'm just an accessory and it doesn't matter how interesting I might be, because he is the footballer and I'm just his wife. I find I get judged a lot as well. It's like 'Are you good enough to be with Ian Woan?' The assumption is that I chased him down in a nightclub because I knew who he was. It's very hard for footballers' wives to get any respect, for people to take you seriously and believe that you met and fell in love like any other couple.

I don't like admitting it, but the groupies did get to me. I'm the type of person that if there is a partnership you do not move in on it – it's hands off. But I was shocked to see how upfront and forward women were when Ian and I went out together. We would be standing together and holding hands, but that didn't matter. They would put numbers in his pocket, grab his butt, whisper in his ear that they would be more than happy to go home with him. It never ceases to amaze me how prepared these women are to degrade themselves. I used to get jealous when we went out. If Ian went up to the bar to get drinks he would be followed, or if I went to the Ladies I'd come back and he'd be surrounded. Once Ian was about to introduce me to this woman when I just saw red: 'I don't care who you are, but just go away and leave us alone.' It transpired she was a friend of a friend. Some of them do give in, and many of them are married, but I think that as women you sort of have to look after each other. You should not go after a married man – I see it as back-stabbing. You wouldn't want it done to you, so don't do it to someone else. Have some class . . .

Right now Ian and I are really happy. He's doing exactly what he wants to do and when it's finished we may go to live in America – it's great to have that choice. I'd be lying if I didn't admit I will miss the social side of being the wife of someone in the limelight. Ian gets invited to all sorts of golfing and charity benefits where we meet some of the weird and wonderful people in the show-business world. But on the other hand, I won't miss those situations where everyone wants a piece of my guy because of what he does and not what he is, and I definitely won't miss the depression, the mood swings that football brings out in Ian. When Ian's career comes to an end, his dream is to be a professional golfer. But I don't mind about that – I'm going to be his caddy . . .

Heather Sanchez

Heather was married to the former Northern Ireland international Lawrie Sanchez. Lawrie scored the winning goal for Wimbledon in the 1988 FA Cup Final and is now first-team coach at the club. Heather was a senior lecturer in art and textile design. She died in August 1998 aged 38.

Lawrie and I had got married in Las Vegas and we'd decided to take in Niagara Falls on our honeymoon. So there we were on a boat, dressed from head to toe in oil-skins when this Englishman approached me. 'Is that your husband?' he said, pointing at Lawrie. 'It's Lawrie Sanchez, isn't it?' and I thought, I can't believe it. We are thousands of miles away from home and this guy is asking me whether the man I've just married is really Lawrie Sanchez. But stupidly I said yes it is, because you do. Then I asked him why he didn't approach Lawrie himself. 'Well, I didn't like to ask him, he's on holiday.' Hey so am I, I thought but then actually just said: 'Well, go and talk to him – he doesn't bite.'

We met at university. I was at Loughborough College of Art and Design doing a degree in textile design and Lawrie was at the university doing a business management degree at the same time as playing football for Reading. I didn't know he was a footballer when I asked him out to a match. Nottingham Forest were playing my team, Liverpool, and I don't think he could believe that a girl was asking him to go to football so we kind of hit it off from the start. He'd never known a woman to start the daily newspaper from the back.

I'd always been interested in football, well, all sport really. I'd played volleyball for the under-16 England team and was very athletic. My dad was a football referee and ran the line at Rochdale, our local club, and my brother Graham was a schoolboy footballer there. He was a big West Ham fan and Bobby Moore was his idol. Dad had followed Burnley when he was young and he often used to take us to football. I can remember spending many afternoons, some of them wet, on the terraces at Old Trafford or on the Kippax at Manchester City's Maine Road ground and when the crowd surged forward, I'd be petrified and thrilled at the same time.

My brother was playing football for Rochdale reserves but there came a time when he had to choose between an education or football. The feeling was that you couldn't do both. In the end Graham chose his education although I am sure he could have studied and played. If only he'd had the support of a manager like Maurice Evans who was Lawrie's boss at Reading Football Club. Maurice respected Lawrie as a footballer but also understood his desire to further himself and so, very unusually, Lawrie combined a degree and a place in the Reading first team. Of course Loughborough was an ideal place to do so because it had a real sports complex with all the facilities, so the balance worked well.

But I think Lawrie found it difficult. If a match didn't go his way or if he wasn't playing particularly well, the crowd would get on his back telling him to get back to university or asking 'Where's your briefcase?' It was the best thing for him but it was hard at the time and not something that's encouraged, even today. I wonder whether one of the reasons is that some football managers think it could be detrimental to the smooth running of the club because the more intellectual a player is, the more likelihood there is of him speaking his mind and challenging, even undermining, the manager.

When I discovered Lawrie was playing for Reading my first question was, where's Reading? I soon found out, as football very much dominated our weekends. I didn't resent that. In fact I always found the adoration of the local people for the players extremely heart-warming. We'd be walking down the street and all these people wanted to talk to the person I was with. The downside was that because he lived and played in Reading, when we socialised we never got away from the football. It was only when we went back to Loughborough and it was just the two of us that Lawrie was no longer the footballer. I learned to balance the two and learned to accept that our supposedly romantic evenings out would often be interrupted by people wanting to talk about the day's game or find out what Lawrie thought about this and that or why he hadn't played well . . .

When Lawrie finished his degree he came back to live in Reading and I went on to do a master's degree at Birmingham University. That was a difficult time because we had been together for three years. Neither of us was expecting our relationship to go anywhere but there must have been something there because we kept in touch and when I finished my studies it was a testing time: it really was make or break to see if we could make the relationship work.

I got a job in the art studio at the *Reading Evening Post* and then ended up in the advertising department. I was head-hunted by another advertising company but I wanted to move back into textile design so I started teaching at Buckinghamshire Chiltern University College where I was also able to do freelance design work such as wall-coverings and greetings cards.

The fact that I had my own life helped as did the fact that we weren't married so we didn't share a surname. Some people treated me differently and wanted to get to know me once they became aware of the football link – especially men. In my advertising job I was often dealing with guys and once they found out about Lawrie and me all they wanted to talk about was football. It was great on one level but to get the job done, I eventually had to nudge them towards the business in hand.

As often happens in football, Maurice Evans suddenly left Reading and the new regime decided to let Lawrie go. He was devastated. Devastated. He had never had to cope with rejection. Swindon came in but then we got a phone call from Dave Bassett, the manager of Wimbledon, who asked Lawrie for a meeting. I thought, well who are Wimbledon? What they were of course was a very unusual club who were in the middle of an unbelievable rise through the divisions. There wasn't and there still isn't another club anywhere like Wimbledon.

At the time Lawrie was just pleased that he was wanted. If he had gone to Swindon it would have been as a swap with another player and he felt he was being thrown out with the bathwater so he chose the London club. I know it must have appeared an odd signing at the time. Wimbledon already had a reputation for playing the long ball game and yet Lawrie had been seen as a cultured player at Reading and in his last season with the third division side had scored ten goals from midfield.

I have to say all that changed when he went to Wimbledon where he became a total and utter long ball player – his skill on the ball, along the ground went out the window. But whatever, they were successful and I don't think Lawrie felt compromised in any way. The Wimbledon motto was to win at any cost and that's what they tended to do. And then of course there was the wonderful spirit at the club, the 'Crazy Gang' spirit which just cannot be bottled.

What I found different about the club was its family atmosphere. They very much took you under their wing – although my first visit to the club was anything but friendly. I had gone into the Wimbledon players' lounge and I couldn't believe how cold everybody was. Nobody came to speak to me and I felt very awkward. It turned out that the lads had been away on some sort of pre-season tour in Spain and the word had got round that some of the girls they had met out there were coming to the game. I was quite tanned at the time and I was blonde and they obviously thought I was one of these groupies so they gave me the cold shoulder. It was only when Lawrie came into the bar after the match and introduced me as his girlfriend that the other players' wives realised that I wasn't competition after all . . .

As well as being a close-knit club Wimbledon have always known how to party and as they continued their rise up to the old first division there was more money, more status, more profile and we all had a ball. The whole thing was like a fairy tale, which of course culminated in the FA Cup Final of 1988.

Nobody expected the team to do anything so they just sailed through the early cup rounds without the slightest pressure but nothing could have prepared us for the media interest once Wimbledon had reached the final, because we had never been involved in football at this level before. The week before our Wimbledon visit was mad, with TV cameras and pressmen everywhere. We did *The Clothes Show* with Jeff Banks and had a splendid makeover. We were dressed by Top Shop . . . Everyone looked super and got into the spirit of it. It didn't matter who was providing the clothes, there was just such a huge party atmosphere and we were swept along by it.

All the wives had arranged to meet up and go on a coach to Wembley together. The lads had stayed overnight in a plush London hotel – very Wimbledon Common as opposed to Wimbledon, Plough Lane, our home ground. But on the Friday evening Dennis Wise had been disappointed to discover that not only were chips off the menu but there was no tomato ketchup either. When they surfaced for breakfast the next morning, every player's table had a shiny new bottle of ketchup on it.

En route to Wembley on the Saturday we met up with the players' coach at Plough Lane, which I believe is quite unusual. I couldn't believe the atmosphere. Everyone was happy and laughing. There were no nerves: they were just enjoying every single minute of it and so were we. We had nothing to lose, but Liverpool, ironically my team, had everything to play for – they were going for the double.

When we reached Wembley all we could see was a sea of red and white. There wasn't a single Wimbledon blue and yellow shirt to be seen. Oh no, we thought. Hide. Our manager Bobby Gould's wife had made us these mascots and they were like little dolls. They had big rosettes pinned to them, big yellow and blue rosettes, and as we walked from our coach towards the stadium we were desperately trying to hide these things from the huge crowd of red and white fans. But despite our efforts we were spotted as Wimbledon and as we were dressed smartly it was obvious we weren't just football fans. It was intimidating and I must admit some of the comments made us apprehensive – suddenly the day turned, slightly. Just for those few minutes walking from the coach to our seats it got a little bit scary because we felt so outnumbered and we realised then that Wimbledon really were the little boys.

It was a scorching hot day and we felt very proud and patriotic singing the National Anthem and there was a special moment when the guest of honour, Princess Diana, was introduced to the players. Suddenly I was amazingly nervous – then the whistle went and I started to relax. There had been a few niggles, but then we won a free kick. Dennis Wise took it and the ball just skimmed off Lawrie's head and into the goal. Everyone around us jumped up but I couldn't work out whether it was Lawrie or Alan Cork who scored. I was watching the referee and it seemed like an eternity before he pointed to the centre spot. It came over the Tannoy that the scorer was Lawrie Sanchez. It was just total, unbelievable euphoria. All the Wimbledon wives were congratulating me, saying, great, Lawrie got the goal. It was so emotional – I couldn't believe it. But of course it didn't end there and I thought, Liverpool are bound to get a goal back. In fact they got a penalty. Dave Beasant, the Wimbledon goalkeeper, had a reputation for saving penalties but as John Aldridge stepped forward to take the spot kick we all had our heads down – we couldn't bear to look and we were saying prayers. But Dave saved the penalty and again we couldn't take it in and until the final whistle went we couldn't believe that Wimbledon were actually going to win the Cup. It wasn't until the players received the trophy and their medals and were running round that it suddenly all began to make sense and to sink in.

The Liverpool players were of course really dejected but we weren't sat near any of their wives. I remember seeing one or two of the Liverpool wives sat just behind the royal box and thinking, huh, they've got seats near the royal box and we're in the cheap seats over here. They'd been there so many times before that the seats probably had Liverpool's name printed on them.

Wimbledon fans were definitely in the minority but it's amazing the number of people I have spoken to since who said they were so pleased we won. They couldn't be seen to be supporting Wimbledon but deep down everyone loves an underdog. Margaret Thatcher sent her congratulations. I suppose Wimbledon's victory was very much what she was all about: that anybody can achieve anything if they put their mind to it and work hard enough – the rise from being a nobody to being top dog.

Because Liverpool had dominated football in the eighties like Manchester United have done in the nineties people were just pleased to see someone different up there lifting the trophy.

But the Liverpool players have never got over it. I recently heard Alan Hansen talking about the day on TV and saying we didn't win, Liverpool just lost. They can't admit, even now, ten years on, that they were beaten. It's obviously still a very sore point.

A party had been laid on for us in the marquee on the pitch at Plough Lane and the BBC came along and did *Match of the Day* from there. No one was celebrating as hard as Lawrie's brother. Just before kick-off he'd put money on Lawrie to score the first goal. The odds were 33–1, which I thought was terrible because Lawrie had quite a good scoring record. Lawrie's brother had laid out £100 . . . Lawrie was so shattered that we decided to go back to the hotel after a few hours, leaving his brother still partying, but not before offering him a place on the celebratory bus ride to the town hall the next day. He didn't turn up, though; nobody saw him for three days.

Everyone was a bit bleary-eyed the next morning and really didn't know how the bus ride would turn out, especially as at first there was nobody on the streets. So we were just partying on the bus all by ourselves when suddenly we turned the corner near the town hall and there was blue and yellow everywhere. Everyone was cheering and we went up to the town hall steps and showed off the Cup. Wimbledon unbelievably had a piece of silverware and everybody wanted to touch it. I was talking to a reporter afterwards who'd been interviewing Lawrie and he asked me if I was Lawrie's wife. 'No,' I said. 'I'm his girlfriend.' When he had gone, Lawrie asked, 'Why did you say that? You should have just said yes.'

'Well, I'm not your wife.'

'You know, I should have proposed to you at Wembley in front of all those people and that would have made it really, really special.'

'It's too late now,' I said. 'You've missed your chance.' But I was gratified that he'd had such a romantic thought even though it was several years later that we actually did get married.

After the Cup Final things changed at Wimbledon. They could no longer be just the lads any more. They suddenly had status and everything became serious. I remember reading the press coverage that day after the FA Cup Final and not one report said that Wimbledon had played well or done a good job. Then they had to move out of Plough Lane which was a lovely, cosy ground but in practical terms when you're in the Premiership you need a bigger ground. We started losing players such as Dave Beasant to Newcastle and suddenly there was almost a new team. Then after a series of managerial changes Joe Kinnear, who had been coaching at the club, took over as manager and it's down to him that the Wimbledon spirit has endured. When Joe took over, I read another article that said Wimbledon had earned the right to be in the Premiership because they'd stuck at it and they'd realised what they are. They will never be a Liverpool or Man United but they're good at what they do and they should be respected for that. It was the only press I've ever read that has been positive about what they have achieved. I've always resented it because when people ask: 'Who does your husband play for?' and I tell them Wimbledon, 'Ohhh Wimbledon,' they say. It's almost like they are still regarded as upstarts.

If you ask football-mad kids what their dream would be they usually say to score the winning goal in a FA Cup Final. Now Lawrie had achieved that dream but I don't

think he realised it until everybody wanted to talk to him.
He was also lucky enough to win three caps playing for
Northern Ireland and he has been fortunate that he has
never had a serious injury in his career. Thank goodness,
because when he broke his collarbone he was a nightmare. It coincided with me taking a study trip of 18-year-
olds to Amsterdam. Foolishly I offered Lawrie the chance
to come with us. It was awful. A hundred teenagers in
Amsterdam and Lawrie behaving like a baby. It was
chaos from start to finish and the final straw was when
Lawrie, who of course was used to being completely cosseted by the club on trips, started to question my role.
Hold on a minute, I told him, when normal people go
away they don't get everything laid on for them – this is
the real world.

I believe very much in fate and the day Lawrie was
offered a job at Sligo Rovers was the day the IRA declared
their first cease-fire in Northern Ireland. His playing
career had finished at Wimbledon and a six-week stay at
Swindon hadn't really worked out. Then out of the blue
the chairman of Sligo invited him to become player-
manager. Their former manager Willie McStay had left to
move to Celtic and the team was in Europe. So when the
job offer came on the same day as the cease-fire I said to
Lawrie, this is telling you you've got to go.

It is beautiful out there, lush, green and peaceful, but
the move was a big upheaval for Lawrie. He asked me to
go with him but I didn't want to give up my job. He only
had a short-term contract and we had two businesses
here and somebody had to run them, so he used to fly
home each week. But he did very well there, only getting
knocked out in the European Cup Winners' Cup by
Bruges who Chelsea then went on to beat.

When I went to Sligo for the first time Lawrie suggested I go shopping across the border as the cease-fire

was still holding. I decided to go to Enniskillen and I hadn't really thought about crossing the border until I came to where the army checkpoint normally was. But they'd all gone and the barriers had gone. I'd driven from the tiny little windy roads in Eire on to the very British straight roads with the familiar street signs and I thought, there's nothing to it. So in the summer after my little boy Jack had been born I decided to repeat the journey with my friend Yvonne, who's from Dublin. Up until then she had always been too nervous to make the border crossing but I had told her how easy it was now and we had a good day out. Then we had just re-crossed the border on our way home when a Land Rover appeared from nowhere and two soldiers got out and slowed the car down. I was so shocked I forgot to put the clutch down and we came to a juddering halt. Suddenly there were guns pointing into the car. We were two women and a baby, and Jack began to cry in the back as the questions started. Where are you going? Where have you come from? Is this your car? Who's your husband? Lawrie Sanchez. Lawrie Sanchez, the manager of Sligo – and the guns disappeared. The power of football. Suddenly everything changed.

Lawrie had been at Sligo Rovers for a season when Wimbledon invited him to come back as their reserve team manager. I'd just had Jack and it made sense. I think the transition was quite difficult because some of the Wimbledon footballers who Lawrie had played with were still there but he did well with the reserves. They won their league and Lawrie was promoted to first-team coach. He is on his way and I think eventually he'd like to manage his own club. I am very proud of Lawrie and I'm still desperately in love with him. We are soul mates and I can't imagine life without him.

Cheryl Hirst

Cheryl Hirst is a trainee solicitor. She is engaged to Andy Booth who began his career at Huddersfield Town and now plays for Sheffield Wednesday.

I was at sixth-form college one day chatting to a friend who was a Huddersfield Town fan. He was showing me some pictures he had of the Town team and then asked me what I liked in a man. I pointed to a picture of Andrew and said: 'He's quite cute.'

I went out and got wrecked on my 18th birthday. I felt absolutely dreadful the next day but my friends and I had arranged to go to the Coliseum, a nightclub in Halifax. So I thought I'd go but not drink and watch them all get wrecked. During the evening my friend came over and said, 'Isn't that the lad over there who you think is quite cute?' It was Andrew. I just walked over, asked him to dance and kissed him and that was it. I hadn't been introduced or anything. It was so unlike me. I wouldn't do it now in a million years. Then we talked all night. He offered to buy me a drink but when we got to the bar he discovered he had no money so I had to buy it and then when we got a taxi home I had to pay again. But we got on so well. He made me laugh and when we said goodbye Andrew gave me the signet ring he was wearing.

Now my dad is a big Huddersfield Town fan and the next morning I told him I had met someone and that his name was Andy Booth. Dad said 'No! Really?' I think Andrew had played once in the first team and was just breaking through into the Town side. I showed off my ring: 'Look what he's given me.' Dad was a bit concerned: 'What's he like?' I reassured Dad that Andrew was a lovely lad and the great thing is that now they are the best of friends and when Sheffield Wednesday haven't got a match they go down together to watch Town play.

When I was a little girl my dad used to drag me along to watch Huddersfield Town – I think I was the son he never had. I stopped going when I was about 14 or 15 when I had to concentrate on my GCSEs, and boys of course. But I was always interested in what Town did. And it was a Town match that was to be the next time I saw Andrew because he had invited me to watch Huddersfield play Scunthorpe in the FA Cup the following Wednesday.

I hadn't been to football for a few years and I couldn't concentrate on the match because I was so scared about meeting Andrew afterwards. He was on the subs' bench and I kept peering down at him. Afterwards he told me that during the match he was talking to the other substitute about how he'd met me and his worst fear was that he wouldn't recognise me when he came out of the players' entrance. You see, he wasn't absolutely wrecked in the nightclub but he'd had a drink and he was dreading not knowing who I was.

Andrew had told me about this other girl who was after him – she was 23. I thought, God, so much competition. Well, it turned out she was at the match that night and that she was an obsessive fan. She would follow him around after every game and bombard him with letters and phone calls. Andrew hated it. Apparently she had latched on to other players before him. Anyway when Andrew and I first started going out she started bad-mouthing me and a couple of weeks after we met she let down all the tyres on Andrew's Renault. The club threatened to ban her. I was only 18 but it didn't bother me – she obviously had her own problems. In the end she just disappeared – she's probably following someone else now. It's not so bad now Andrew is at a Premiership club. I think when footballers are at smaller clubs they are more accessible to their fans and this sort of thing can happen.

I was still at school studying for my A levels and I had been accepted to do a history degree at Leicester University. But I'd fallen completely and madly in love with Andrew. So I said, 'I'm not going to university.' We'd only been going out with each other a few months and I was convinced that we would split up if we went our separate ways. In the end I stayed at home and switched to taking a law degree at Huddersfield University.

Once I had my degree I then had to take a legal practice course to become a solicitor. It cost £5,500 for a year's study. At first I was going to get a loan but the interest was colossal. Being a footballer, even if only at Huddersfield Town, Andrew had saved a bit of money and he said, 'Let me pay for you.' I had friends who had to take out loans and they were in a real mess when they finished because if they didn't get a job at the end, and some of them didn't, they were saddled with all that debt. I really did feel the strain and I don't know how I could have got through it without Andrew. We had moved in together but he washed and cooked and cleaned – the only thing he didn't do was the ironing. My friends can't believe he's a footballer because he's so down to earth. He has nine good grades at GCSE but left school at 16 to become a footballer. When he's 35 and his career is finished I'll have a good job to look after him. But at the moment he looks after me. When I come home every night my tea is on the table – every night it's there. Andrew trains two hours a day whereas I set off at 7 a.m. every day and get back at half past six, so why not?

As a striker he is under a certain amount of pressure to deliver. I sit with his mum at the games and we always sit in our lucky seats. When Andrew scores we both jump up and shout around. It's a wonderful feeling of elation.

But my philosophy is that he doesn't need to score as long as he plays well. While Andrew was doing so well at Town we were aware that Leeds and Liverpool scouts were watching him and Southampton were also apparently interested, but he was never told. After the end of the season when Town were promoted to the first division we went on holiday to Cyprus and while we were there we got engaged. We arrived home on the Friday to be told me had to call the Huddersfield secretary and from there everything happened really quickly. Andrew met representatives from Sheffield Wednesday and signed everything that night. His transfer fee was £2.65 million. If that wasn't enough, on that very same day I found out I had gained a good law degree.

When I went to my first match at Sheffield Wednesday the atmosphere was amazing and going away to clubs like Manchester United brought home to me the fact that Andrew was now playing against the best footballers in the country. I love going to away matches. It's a real family occasion. There's about ten of us from my and Andrew's family and we often stop off for lunch and always have a good day out – except when Wednesday lose. Andrew likes me to go. Every now and again I say I might go shopping today but he always wants me to watch and tell him how I think he's done. In his first season at Sheffield Wednesday, Andrew went three or four games without scoring so he got out a video of all the goals he scored for Huddersfield and watched it on the Saturday morning before the match. He scored thirty-odd goals in his last season at Town but stepping up to the Premiership was definitely moving on to a different level. Amazingly, it worked. He scored. And now it's become a superstition with him and he watches the video of himself scoring goals before every game.

On the odd occasion that Sheffield Wednesday are

playing miles away Andrew's mum and dad work on the turnstiles at town along with his grandad who's in his eighties. It's a family thing and now football is part of my family too. Even my mum is a convert. She went to watch a match several years ago thinking she was going to hate it. We won and I think Andrew scored and ever since then she hasn't missed a game. And my grandma tunes into the football on the radio every Saturday and when we go to see her she always talks about football first.

Sheffield Wednesday are a very homely club and Andrew is very happy there. Every now and again there is something glamorous to attend such as *The Full Monty* première party. There was the red carpet and the cameras flashing and I thought to myself, This is the life, but of course it's not. We just go to town on a Saturday night and have a drink with our friends and then out for a curry. Maybe it's different in London.

Kirstine Fry

Kirstine is the wife of Barry Fry, one of football's most colourful characters, who took Barnet into the Football League before managing Southend, Birmingham City and now Peterborough United.

Barry had separated from his wife and needed someone to help him with his children, Jane and Mark, on a holiday he had booked. He knew my mother and my name came up. We went out twice before the holiday to see if we got on. It was Mr Fry – all very formal. It was only when we came home and he moved out of the area that he asked me out for a date. It was a very different situation and there was an instant attraction between us – and he hasn't changed from the day I met him. On our second date we went to a football dinner and even then he was incredibly attentive. We must have been in the dreamy phase – we couldn't take our eyes off each other.

When I met Barry he'd just become the manager of non-league Barnet. My dad is Scottish and supports Hearts and my two brothers are football fans but I never took any notice. Well, that is apart from Kenny Dalglish. I have his picture on the fridge because I've always liked Kenny. He seems such a lovely family man and there's never any scandal and of course, like me, he's Scottish. But football meant very little to me.

Barry's always been involved in football. He was a very promising young player with Manchester United and he played for England Schoolboys. He was dedicated but as he got older other interests such as gambling and the dogs got in the way and he never quite made it. In fact if he couldn't be a footballer he wanted to be a professional gambler or mastermind one of the biggest crimes of the century – pit his wits against something impossible. He just loves a challenge.

After five or six years we got married and Barry

moved to become manager of Maidstone FC. We'd just signed the papers selling our house when he was sacked. It was terrible, but Barnet wanted him back so we moved house again, this time to Bedford. Barnet always struggled money-wise even though the players were only on about £20 a week. So we used to open the clubhouse to raise money. There was a bingo night and on a Friday we organised a disco and served behind the bar. At 11 p.m. I would pull the shutters down and Barry would put them back up again. He wouldn't shut up until the last person who had any money to spend had spent it. Then it was time to clean up and we'd be mopping the floor sometimes as late as three in the morning.

If there was an away game we'd be up early to drive to the ground and then straight back again to Barnet to open up for the Saturday disco – then I'd spend Sunday washing the kit. It was hard work but Barry and I were always together and I loved those times. You know what they say about the hungry years. If we went back now it would be difficult, with the children, but they were good times.

Once the cash flow situation was so bad we had to wait very late one night until a guy came down to empty all the machines in the bar so we could pay the players. Things were very tight. Barry went for weeks without getting paid but there were only two of us, although of course he also had to look after his children. We got married on a Friday – but on the Thursday night Barry asked if I would sign this paper. It was a second mortgage on the house. The money was needed to pay the brewery so Barnet could open up the social club the next day. No money, a second mortgage . . . but I believed in Barry totally, I always have. I don't ever feel threatened even though he is in one of the most insecure jobs there is.

When Adam, our eldest, was on the way, we went six

weeks without money. Then Stan Flashman became involved in Barnet and things took a turn for the better. Barry and Stan formed a very successful partnership and they took Barnet into the Football League but Flashman turned out to be a real Jekyll and Hyde. He always treated me perfectly well but I often heard him screaming down the phone at Barry. However, it didn't put him off and Barry named our second child Amber after the Barnet shirt colours – amber and black. I should have guessed then how much football was part of Barry's life.

There's no doubt that our lives do revolve around football even to the extent of Barry buying me flowers. He always wanted to treat me but because he was coming home late at night from a football match or scouting he'd buy the last of the roses in the petrol station or the paper shop and they'd be dead by the morning. I said, no more flowers – but the thought was there.

When I was pregnant with Anna-Marie, my younger daughter, Barry was managing Barnet. They were playing Brentford at home when my contractions started and of course Barry was at the game. So I asked Adam to ring his dad and tell him to come home as soon as possible. After the match Barry told the waiting reporters that he couldn't stop to chat as he had to dash off to deliver a baby and cut the cord – which he did. When I left the hospital the next day I hadn't rung anybody and I took Anna-Marie to my mum and dad's house as a surprise. But when I got there they knew all about it. Her birth had been announced on Teletext along with the match result, which I remember was an incredible 5–5.

I'm best when I forget about the match, and I can tell by the way Barry shuts the car door whether he's won or lost. Or failing that the way he says hello to Basil our dog when he comes in the front door. I don't get involved in football so I don't get the pressure. But I know when

Barry's feeling it so I just pick up after him, his discarded shoes and so on, rather than letting off steam. It's like dealing with the children misbehaving. You know when you should make allowances.

Barry's public persona is this charming and larger-than-life character and that is exactly how he is with me. Once a TV programme followed him around at work and the revelation to me was what went on inside the dressing room. I'd always wanted to be a fly on the wall. In one scene he goes mad for a split second and then calms down immediately and that is just how he is at home. He has a wonderful relationship with the children – they never talk to each other, though, they just shout. I don't think anyone really dislikes him. There's no real in-between – you either love him or hate him, and I do both.

At home he certainly isn't a handyman – it's like he has boxing gloves on if he tries anything DIY. He has no interest in the house whatsoever. He could sit in a shack and he'd be happy with his chair, TV, remote control and phone. Once a reporter came to the house and halfway through the interview Barry said he needed to shave but was quite happy to continue the chat upstairs in the bathroom even though I'd just had another baby and there were clothes everywhere . . .

After all those years at Barnet, Barry was sacked by recorded delivery. It then came up on Teletext. Fortunately Southend asked him to be their manager and after a successful spell there he moved on to Birmingham City. He felt that this was the chance he'd been waiting for. Birmingham City is a sleeping giant of a football club. The combination of Barry, David Sullivan, the owner, and Karen Brady, a woman chief executive, kept Birmingham's name in the papers, as did Barry's regular buying of strikers.

Adam used to go to Birmingham City with Barry all

the time and he took it particularly badly when his dad was eventually sacked from there. Barry couldn't believe it either – he'd been out only the night before with the other major investors in the club, the Gold brothers. They hadn't said a word to him. Barry doesn't hold grudges so he phoned David Sullivan to say thanks for the chance to manage Birmingham. But my first thought was for Adam and I said we should go to meet him from school and tell him together. Adam, who was about 10 or 11, didn't seem too bad until we got home but when he read the news on Teletext he cried his eyes out. His bedroom was all done out in Birmingham posters and colours and he ripped everything down.

Both Adam and my younger son Frank want to be footballers. The discipline is good for them and it's much better than hanging around street corners. I also think that taking a couple of years from 15 and 16 years old to have a go at being a footballer is no bad thing, as long as they realise they can go back to studying if they don't make it. Adam wants to play for Manchester United and Frank for Arsenal. I was chatting to Frank one day and I said: 'You'll probably be wanting to drive as soon as you're 17, won't you?'

'No, Mum, I won't be here,' he replied. 'I'll have signed for Arsenal by then and I'll be living in my own flat in London.'

'What if you're not good enough?'

'Then I'll play for Peterborough.'

'Dad won't sign you if you're not good enough.'

'Well, I'll be normal, then.'

Peterborough is where Barry is manager now. That brought difficulties with it too at first because Barry also bought into the club and then discovered that a lot of half-truths had been told. Fortunately it's all been sorted out. A local businessman, Peter Boizot, the man behind Pizza Express, has since bought the club. He isn't football-minded but he's really keen for the club to do well for the town's sake. He became well-known nationally with his £100,000 sponsorship of a Royal Academy exhibition. We went to London for the opening and Barry was asked what he thought of the paintings. He replied: 'They'd look nice around the swimming pool.'

Brigitte Arscott

Brigitte is the fiancée of Southampton footballer John Beresford, whom she met when he was playing for Newcastle United. She trained as a beautician and aerobics teacher and now works as a personal trainer.

The letter from a 17-year-old girl fan started: 'John, I love your fabulous blue eyes, your long, lovely blond hair,' and I thought, oh yes, here we go, dreading what was coming next. I needn't have worried. She finished: 'You remind me of my pet budgie.' You see I often help John with his fan mail and you do get some odd ones. 'When you bend over, I quiver,' began another but this time it was from a lad, which did make John feel a little uncomfortable. Then there was another woman, old enough to be John's mother, who obviously thought I wasn't doing my 'job' and wrote offering to come and look after him.

When I met John he was about to sign for Newcastle United and he tried to explain to me exactly what it meant to be a footballer – particularly how fanatical the fans were on Tyneside. It's a big, big part of their lives. I didn't actually move in with him until he'd been at Newcastle for some time and despite everything he'd told me I found it really strange that everyone knew who he was. I didn't know what to do and I felt quite embarrassed and then John felt embarrassed for me. Fans, particularly young lads, used to come up to him in the streets and ask him if he was John Beresford and I would just walk off. I didn't want to stand there and be given the look-over, especially if there were any girls in the group as they'd often be looking at you like death. It made me feel uncomfortable. As for the men, they'd just ignore me completely. Once we arrived at a charity ball and the host greeted John warmly, congratulating him on his most recent game, laughing and joking. Not a word was addressed to me, not even a hello.

I also found that in some people's eyes just being with John made me a bit of a celebrity and I know some of my personal training clients used to say: 'We'd better clear the table, Brigitte's coming.' But I think most people do enjoy a little bit of limelight so when Tyne Tees TV approached John and me with the idea of filming the last few weeks of my pregnancy with Billy, I agreed. Each week we would feature on their local programme – we were filmed at ante-natal classes, at the gym and with Billy live on the show when he was three days old. It was good fun to do and I think it showed viewers that a footballer's home life is just like their own.

I first met John when he came to stay at the health farm where I was working. He came to one of my fitness classes and then later on in the week I met him again for an aromatherapy treatment. Everything was very professional – I suppose we were just talking shop. Then on my night off I went to the local village with some of the girls and we bumped into him in a pub. Management probably wouldn't have been very happy if they'd known we were fraternising with the guests but it just happened and we got on really well – I suppose it was fate.

When I went to matches at Newcastle I did feel the onus was on me to play the football wife, to dress up a bit, but it really depended on what mood I was in and of course I had my children Jay and Billy with me. There was a time when John used to bring all his problems home. If he was injured or dropped from the team, he would be irritable and inevitably we would end up having a big ding-dong. But as he's got older he's learned to cope, and having the children has definitely helped. Now when he walks through the door, no matter what mood he's in, Billy and Jay make him laugh.

On match days John likes to follow a set routine – a bit of a lie-in, Weetabix, then toast and jam mid-morning. We definitely do not practise abstinence on the Friday night but I know a lot of the lads are superstitious and maybe if they aren't doing so well they might experiment . . .

I found Kevin Keegan a really friendly, family man who always took time out to say hello to us and ask after the children. So I couldn't believe it when John and Keegan had their famous slanging match which resulted in John being substituted during a televised game. Millions of people supposedly saw John rather colour-fully disagreeing with some instructions that came from the manager on the bench. Of course I heard John's side of the story and then read a completely different version in the papers. Obviously it's important to have a good relationship with the media but when I read the points awarded to each player for their performance the day after the match, I sometimes wonder just what game the journos have been watching.

Sometimes I feel, because I'm not that interested in football and don't watch if John isn't playing, that I don't appreciate how good a player he is. But when he won Newcastle Utd Player of the Year I was so proud. It was a great shame when he had to leave Newcastle.

In fact, Kevin Keegan was well on his way to finalising an extension to John's contract which would have kept us at Newcastle for three more seasons. Then Keegan sud-denly left, to be replaced by Kenny Dalglish and the Newcastle board made it clear that they planned to sell John. It was also obvious that the great Newcastle spirit, which had made the team so popular around the country when Keegan was in charge, was waning. It was all a bit unsettling for John. We heard rumours that Sheffield United and Derby were interested in buying him but they didn't have the funds available. Anyway we put our flat on the market as we were finally moving into a barn we had been converting in John's home city of Sheffield, and that day we arrived home to find a message on the answer machine that Southampton wanted to speak to him. So he quickly packed a bag and caught a flight down to Eastleigh airport, stopping off at the Newcastle physio's house to pick up his medical records. Southampton were playing Everton at Goodison on the Saturday and they wanted John to travel with them, so he signed and ended up having a medical at 10 p.m. that night. It was so quick. That was it. He'd gone.

The Southampton move has been great for John. There is a good atmosphere at the Dell and Dave Jones, the manager, has worked miracles since he has been there. We still live in Sheffield and John travels down to Southampton each week with fellow Yorkshire exiles Carlton Palmer and David Hirst who also play for the South Coast club.

I have been steadily gaining my personal training qualifications and I'm determined to have a career. I know I don't have to pay the bills and many people, including John, think I'm mad but I supported myself for so long that I would miss my independence, and anyway there's only so much talking you can do to the children.

We're fortunate in that our ambitions for life after football are similar. John has also studied for his personal fitness trainer exams and one idea we have is to open a mini health farm where you can come for the day, for beauty treatments and fitness classes. But while John is still playing I am going to take up the training again for my sporting goal – winning the British Aerobics Championship. I was well on my way to achieving the high level of fitness needed for entry into this competition when I fell pregnant with Jay. But I'm determined to have another go. We are getting married in June 1999 and it would be wonderful if I could lift my own trophy as well ...

Lorraine Sass

Lorraine Sass is an actress who regularly appears on stage and TV. Her partner David Campbell is a former Northern Ireland international who now runs the David Campbell Celebrity Soccer Schools.

I met David when he was playing for Nottingham Forest and I was in a play at the Nottingham Playhouse. I didn't know anything about football and didn't know who he was at all. He did tell me he'd just come back from the World Cup in Mexico, where he had been playing for Northern Ireland, so I thought he must be quite a good player. He came to see me in a play called *Stags and Hens* which was a great show for me because it was set in Liverpool, where I'm from, so a lot of my friends were in it and we had a great giggle.

David and I met through the woman who was on the stage door. One of the girls in the show didn't have a boyfriend and so we set about the task of finding her a man. We asked this stage door lady if she knew any nice men in Nottingham. 'Well, actually,' she said, 'I do. My parents run a lodging house for young footballers,' and she gave us the telephone number of the house where David was staying. I thought it was outrageous that my friend actually phoned up a man she had never met, but she did. Then, when the landlady told her he was out, she left a message and amazingly, David rang back.

Anyway, I'd just made this huge chocolate cake and we decided to invite him round for coffee and cake. He has never lived it down because I just thought, what kind of a man is it that gets a phone call from a woman he's never heard of, inviting him round for coffee, and then actually turns up? Unfortunately, or perhaps fortunately, he liked me a little bit more than my friend. Maybe it was my chocolate cake – he still loves it.

I don't think David had ever been to the theatre when

he came to watch our show, just as I hadn't ever been to a football match. Football and acting have so much in common, though. There's the applause and the plying of your trade in front of an audience, exposing yourself and having to work with the pressure that you might make a mistake. Both can look fantastic and there is a certain amount of glamour attached to them. But everything that is ever achieved in either of the two fields is down to sheer hard graft.

I think David found me unusual because I wasn't the sort of groupie who would be hanging around the Forest boys. I knew so little about football but when David mentioned the World Cup in Mexico I suddenly recalled seeing an item about him on *News at Ten*. He'd celebrated his 21st birthday when he was in Guadalajara and Pat Jennings, the Northern Ireland goalkeeper, was 41 at the same time so they were both presented with a commemorative cake on the team bus, and I remember thinking isn't that great. Then just a few months later here was this man I'd seen on television, pursuing me around the theatres of England with flowers, letters and phone calls. He completely denies all this now, of course.

The show I was working in when we met got a great deal of publicity in Nottingham so when, shortly after we got together, David and I were photographed at a local night club, I automatically presumed that the woman had recognised me. Then I realised she was only taking a shot when my back was turned to her – she was taking a picture of David, not me. That put me in my place but it was part of my growing understanding of how important football is to people and I have come to love what soccer gives to fans rather than the game itself. I now appreciate why people enjoy football and the sense of camaraderie and belonging it gives them.

As well as being pursued by David, I was absolutely

fascinated by him. He had such an unusual lifestyle but one which in many respects reflected my own as an actress. The fact that you could be in the right place at the right time and land a contract that could totally transform your life. By the same token you could be at the top of the tree one moment and then nobody wants to know you the next. One of the things that interested me about David was that on one level he seemed so worldly-wise for a 21-year-old – he'd been all over the world playing for Northern Ireland and Nottingham Forest – but in other respects he was almost childlike because so much was being done for him on a day-to-day basis. He was completely ignorant of things like shopping and cooking, which I found quite endearing. The atmosphere at football clubs often resembles the cosseted environment of a nursery and it didn't surprise me at all when Brian Clough, David's manager, used to put a box full of chocolate bars on the team coach as a treat. Sweeties from the manager was really good for morale – it was extraordinary.

David is from Northern Ireland and he had a lot to deal with coming to live in England at just 16 years old. He was put in a lodging house with a lot of other teenage boys, which I'm sure was tremendous fun: I'd have liked to have been a fly on the wall. But he was also away from his family and was already having to deal with the pressure to succeed. I know that a lot of people think footballers have it laid on a plate but there's a lot more to it than that. They have so much to deal with – especially nowadays with the massive amounts of money involved. It's no surprise that the really high-profile players can be so nervous about everything. You imagine that they've got it all and that they are living the kind of life that everybody else just dreams about, but so few of them seem to be able to appreciate it. That can't be right. I always said to David that he wouldn't appreciate his career until it was over and I think that's true for most players.

My career also began when I was very young. I started going to dance lessons when I was five. Then when I was 11 I saw an advert for a charm school and I decided that was for me. Elocution lessons were part of the tuition and I began drama classes. It was also a modelling agency and I did a lot of child modelling too. So there were similarities in my own and David's background even down to the relationship with your friends and family when, because you are in the spotlight, a lot of their dreams and ambitions are lived through you.

My first professional job was as Bill the Badger in the *Rupert Bear Show* in Jersey. I couldn't believe someone was paying me to have such a good time and I had my own Toy Town fan club. Like David, I had quite a lot of success early on. I did a long-running TV series called *How We Used To Live* which was nominated for a BAFTA. I played Alice Selby, one of the leads. I've done quite a lot of TV, including *A Touch of Frost*, *EastEnders* and *City Central*, and I was also in the controversial National Theatre production of *The Romans in Britain*. I was 21 at the time but I was playing a 13-year-old. One of the scenes, which featured a homosexual rape, had attracted a lot of press attention and that was my first real taste of press hounding. The controversy reached the letters pages of the newspapers. One singled me out saying, adults fine, they're old enough to make their own decisions and moral judgements, but a young girl at such an impressionable age – well, her parents should be hung. We were told not to speak to anyone and I arrived at the theatre that night to be greeted by the massed ranks of the press and TV. It was then that I thought to myself: I've made it. Here I was walking through the stage door of the National Theatre saying 'No comment.' I loved it.

I'd not been going out with David for too long when Nottingham Forest beat my father's team Everton and David won Man of the Match. This didn't go down well at home. In fact they weren't at all impressed I was seeing a footballer. I think they thought, we know the type – a real womaniser with his brains in his feet, who wears a white shell suit and has permed hair. Remember, we lived in Liverpool. In fact David got 12 O levels but of course had to leave school to become a professional footballer. Yet all through his career he utilised the subsidised courses on offer from the Professional Footballers' Association to learn other skills. However, this didn't prevent him going through what we now call his 'mid-life crisis' at just 25 when we separated for a year.

It all began with David getting a serious knee injury. I'm sure most footballers' partners say the same thing: that once a player is injured they believe the whole world should come out in sympathy. It was a cruciate ligament injury and David felt at the time that to regain his fitness he had to devote all his time, energy and mental stimulus to getting over it. So we went from having a blissfully happy relationship to not having one at all. He told me that long term we would be together but at that time there could be no distractions. I found this very difficult to come to terms with because I felt I had always been a supportive partner. We laugh about it now but it was a shock at the time because it was completely out of the blue. Once the injury crisis was over he called me and we got back together. I was quite cool to begin with but I've always believed we were so right for each other and that we are a great team. I don't think that even now he fully understands what happened. But I'm sure it's because the football profession is so demanding that the quest to regain his fitness just took over and he became obsessed with it.

Well, I suppose I did get some sort of revenge with the pink rabbit incident. David had been abroad playing football and rang me to say he was on his way home and could I please meet him at Manchester airport. Fine, I thought. Then he added the proviso that I should look nice. Cheeky beggar, I thought. I'll show him. So I nipped down to the local haberdashery and bought masses of bright pink furry material, went home and fashioned an entire rabbit outfit, complete with wire ears. I drove off to the airport and then made a quick change before strolling up and down the concourse dressed as a pink rabbit – oh, and I had pink glasses on that squirted water. I got quite a lot of attention – two guys were even trying to chat me up, when I saw David. He was looking forlornly around for me as people who had obviously recognised him were approaching him for a chat. Then he had this sudden realisation that I was the pink rabbit and he actually tried to walk away. I was having none of that and made him walk all the way back to the car with me in tow. He was mortified – but he has never asked me to look 'nice' again.

I'm seven years older than David and I think that has helped our relationship enormously. I was often away on tour and after a game David would be straight on to whatever motorway took him to wherever I might happen to be at the time. I think that kept our relationship fresh. It was good for him to get away from the football environment. Sometimes if we went out with the other players, after a defeat people would come up to them and have a go, or if they'd done well then they'd try and monopolise them. There was very little let-up apart from when we were safely tucked away in our own home. So that whereas before I met David I, like many people, thought footballers led this whirl of a social life I was learning that often it's very different than one imagines.

It was always me trying to get David to go out to a disco to let off steam.

When David was at Charlton the team hadn't played very well and they lost the match. Afterwards one of the wives said she really wished her husband was a bricklayer. I thought, what an odd thing to say. But I suppose if you crave security and order and you want to know where you're going to be in five years' time, then you would be better off married to a bricklayer. In this respect I have perhaps been able to help David because I never desired a regular lifestyle and often had to find alternative employment when the acting work went quiet. So when David had his next serious injury, and this time it was *really* serious, I knew we had to start looking for something new. His leg was severely broken – the doctors said it was more like a motorbike accident.

How I found out about it was just horrendous. I was in Liverpool and was listening out for the football results when I heard David's game had been delayed. I immediately thought, oh that's because someone has been injured. I hope it's not David. When I got home there was an answerphone message saying: 'We're very sorry. David's in hospital. He's had an accident. We'll phone you later' – and that was it. No contact number, not even the name of the hospital. All I knew was that he was playing in London so I dialled 192 and got the phone numbers of all the hospitals in London and then just called round until I found him. I realised almost as soon as I saw him that this time it was career-threatening, but being the positive person I am, I told him: 'Right, this is a great opportunity', to which he replied, 'A great opportunity – I feel like I'm dying.'

So I went away and I sat at the computer for about three weeks formulating the plan for the David Campbell Celebrity Soccer Schools. Then I presented it to various businesspeople and sports manufacturers and they came beating a path to our door and we haven't really looked back since then. I knew that there were plenty of soccer schools about but this idea was very different and was based on utilising David's contacts among the footballers who had finished in football proper and were twiddling their thumbs. In some respects it gives them back a little of their former glory because we promote their achievements and when they arrive in a town everyone's delighted to see them.

The soccer schools run in England, Eire and Northern Ireland and we're hoping to expand into the USA with a franchising operation. We also have an event management company and we're planning to set up an agency which will nurture young up-and-coming talent. What is interesting are the attitudes I come across as a woman getting actively involved in soccer. Sometimes at meetings people will assume I am David's secretary. When that happens and I eventually sign a deal with them I usually stick an extra nought on the end . . .

As a female I've been able to bring a fresh, new approach to our business. I don't think you have to know all the intricacies of the game – the offside rule, for instance – to be able to contribute. At the Celebrity Soccer Schools we actively encourage girls to come on the courses, which always finish with a Penalty Prince *and* Princess prize.

I continue to act but also work in all areas of the business. As we do a lot of our courses in Ireland, last summer we hired a cottage and I stayed there with about eight former international footballers as the general cook and dogsbody. I had a wonderful time. What amazed me was that they'd be coaching all day then they would come back to their cottage at about four o'clock, change straight into their football kit and then all go out training.

I'd get the food cooked and I'd be at the door calling: 'Boys, boys, come on in for your dinner,' but I could never get them to come in because they'd be having these competitions. They'd set themselves courses or agility trials and as some of them were not quite as fit as they used to be in their prime they would be struggling, but they were still so competitive, they just couldn't stop. I had a few burned dinners but I lived the atmosphere and I got a sense of what it must have been like at a club, in the dressing room and so on – the whole 'skitting', we call it in Liverpool, the whole banter between them.

So out of a dreadful moment in David's career something very positive was born. I suppose I have Pollyanna instincts – I think everything will turn out wonderful in the end and that's one of the ways I feel I have contributed to David's career: I wasn't just an appendage. I may not have been on the field with him but I did help him to get in the right frame of mind. If David ever chose to take a break from business he would make the most terrific manager because I do think he has a genuine understanding of players' needs and if he ever went into that field I would love to have some involvement. As a trained dancer it always amazes me that footballers do not do more stretching, so I'd make them all take ballet classes with me. But I think my most important role would be to take each player out to tea from time to time. We would have a little heart-to-heart and I just think that this would make so much difference to their confidence and the team spirit. Yes, I definitely think David and I would be a winning managerial team.

Suzi Walker

Suzi Walker is married to Tottenham Hotspur goal-keeper, Ian Walker. The former model presented Hiya! *on cable TV, interviewing fellow footballers' wives.*

I met Ian on a blind date set up by another player, Jason Cundy, who now plays for Ipswich. I used to do some modelling work with Jason's wife Lizzy and Ian spotted one of my promotional cards at their flat. Apparently he thought I looked all right and asked my friend to arrange a date. Ian was in Tottenham's reserves then and not very well known, so my first question was: 'What does he look like?' I was assured he was really good looking. I had this idea that most footballers were arrogant, cocky bastards and basically I thought he was going to be a pig. But I was having problems with a former boyfriend and I thought I'd go along for a laugh. So when he rang I arranged to meet him and then started going through all the magazines trying to find a picture of him.

When it came to the date I just didn't feel like it but I didn't have his phone number so, not wanting to stand him up, I pulled on a pair of jeans and went to meet him at this bar. Guess what? He was over an hour late. Typical, I thought. I was steaming and was just about to go when he turned up. As soon as I saw him I swore at him: 'Bastard, bloody cheek.' Then I realised I didn't even know for sure that it was him and even as I was saying it I realised he looked a real dish. I had managed to find a small clipping but he was so much better in the flesh – my ideal man.

We got on really well together but at the end of the date I didn't think anything would come of it. He was nice looking but I wasn't that bothered. I think initially Ian was more smitten with me than I was with him. He rang the next day but I still didn't have any great expectations of the relationship developing. I had fallen for his looks but I was wary because I knew what footballers could be like – just wanting to have a good time. But Ian wasn't like that. Indeed that first night he was sweet and shy and I did most of the talking.

My family are into rugby. They hated football and still do although they are now proud of Ian. My grandparents lived near Highbury and when I was little I used to say I supported Arsenal but I wasn't really that interested. My brother played rugby for England Colts and Harlequins. So I had never watched football and knew nothing about it and I think Ian liked that. I wasn't thinking, ooooh, I'm meeting Ian Walker. He wasn't that well known and I certainly didn't know who he was. Most girls seem to think footballer equals money. That wasn't the case when I met Ian. He didn't even have a car. I was always lending him money and my car. If we went out to dinner I paid, and when we first moved in together it was a very ordinary place and I never dreamt that within a short space of time we'd have such a lovely home. But still people think I only married him for his money – it really aggravates me.

When I was a little girl I was always putting on shows in the cul-de-sac where we lived and I loved the TV series *Fame*. My dad is in show business. He used to play the saxophone professionally; now he manages the Johnny Howard Band and organises functions in the West End and for the royal family. He didn't want me to get involved in the business, but I just kept saying 'Please, please', so when I was 12 I went to the Italia Conti stage school. I started doing TV commercials: one was for milk and another for an Iron Maiden record compilation. I got a small part in the TV series *Hide Away* and was in a Musical Youth video. I also made the covers of teen magazines *My Guy* and *Oh Boy*. Then when I left school I did a summer season singing and dancing in Monte Carlo. I was only 16 and it was very hard work for very little money. I was homesick too. Looking back, I should have enjoyed myself more as a young teenager. Being in show business I was always worrying about my appearance. In fact, when I was 13 I was a bit anorexic. I don't think I would let my daughter go on the stage. I wouldn't want her to face that pressure.

When I came home from working abroad I was out of touch with the entertainment world so modelling seemed to be the answer. It was relatively easy and paid good money but I didn't enjoy it. If the girls weren't bitchy they were pretentious. As I'm five-foot-five I couldn't do cat-walk modelling so it was mostly advertising and lingerie. Then it was suggested I should try Page 3, you know, the *Sun*. My dad nearly had a heart attack and begged me not to do it. But I felt it was my life and anyway, didn't I go topless on the beach – what's the difference? It was all pretty harmless and I drew the line at full frontal stuff.

In fact I only did Page 3 about four times. It is just a small part of my portfolio but now it is a millstone around my neck. If my name ever gets mentioned in print it's usually 'Suzi Walker, Page 3 model'. I think, oh no, not that again. I don't regret going topless. I didn't have a problem with it and I still don't, but other people do and I've become branded by it.

I stopped the glamour modelling when I met Ian. He was a little jealous and I can understand that. He some-times does photo shoots and I certainly wouldn't want him having to snuggle up to some beauty with very little on. But that of course severely restricted the work a small blonde model can do and the work fizzled out. Then out of the blue I was offered a presenter's job on *Sportstalk*, a cable TV show. It was a live monthly show where I visited the homes of other footballers' wives and interviewed them. I was completely thrown in at the deep end, and at first I was terrible. But I did enjoy it and it meant I could keep my own identity and earn my own money. That's important to me. I like my independence.

When I was wondering whether to go on the blind date with Ian, my friend Lizzy told me he had been voted the Sexiest Footballer of the Year. But it was only when I became involved with him that I realised just how much of a sex symbol he was. I suppose that was when I started getting paranoid and insecure about our relationship. By this time Ian had become the Spurs first-team goalkeeper and he began to hang out with all the established players. He was always being asked for his autograph and we began going to some really quite high-profile bashes.

It just freaked me out. I suddenly thought, if he's mixing with all these famous people, what does he want with me, what's he doing with me? This awful feeling of insecurity led to us splitting up. It was a terrible time, especially as Ian had a few flings. I thought, sod you, I don't want you back. One of the flings made the newspapers and my dad desperately tried to hide it from me. But I saw it and it broke my heart. Then Ian started to ring but I refused to take his calls. After two weeks he turned up on my parents' doorstep and when I saw him I knew the love was still there. When we'd first met we saw each other every day for a year and I think it was all too intense. Too much, too soon. Shortly after we got back together we went on holiday and Ian proposed. I thought, if he wants to marry me it must be true love.

When I see him on the pitch I always think I'd love to go right up close to him because he looks so different – is that really you? It's the same when he's on TV. The whole aspect of Ian Walker, the famous footballer, being recognised still freaks me out when we're out shopping. I just think you should see him at home – particularly when he wears his little hat. But when he does go out with his tracksuit and hat on he still gets spotted. It's amazing, but I'm learning to adapt to this goldfish-bowl side of things. At the very beginning Ian warned me that we could never have words in public. I thought, don't give it the large one, but it's true. He is seen as public property by some fans and the female fans are the worst. They showed it on that Channel 4 *Cutting Edge* programme I was involved in. They interviewed some girls outside a club we'd been to and they were talking about Ian as if he was free and available even though they had seen him with me. All those girls hovering around him – it aggravates me so much that we tend not to go out to clubs any more.

And if they're not after him they're after me. It's that feeling that all of a sudden everyone wants to be your friend. People ring up all the time and I know it's only because I'm married to a famous footballer. For God's sake, I think. There's so many hangers-on who just don't take no for an answer, but keep pestering you for tickets and favours. Ian's very patient and always very polite but they don't take the hint. We keep changing the phone number, but somehow they find it and when I hear the telephone ringing it wears me down. Honestly, they are worse than the groupies. Sometimes I can't bear it so we get away for a few days and I breathe a huge sigh of relief – thank God we're away from all those false people.

You are also aware of petty jealousies. If someone won the lottery you'd be pleased for them. Why can't people be happy about our good fortune? I've had people come round to see the house and afterwards they just don't comment, or they pick holes in it. The public don't seem to mind artists in the show-business world earning a lot of money, but some fans moan that footballers earn too much. But footballers have a skill just like a songwriter or a singer and they work really hard at it and put up with so much mental pressure. Ian cares so much. It's nothing to do with money for him. He plays because he loves football, he loves Tottenham. I used to get a lot of stick because he'd have this smile on his face when a goal went past him into the net. I used to say, 'Please Ian, don't do that,' but it was a subconscious thing – you know if you don't laugh, you'll cry, sort of thing. He tries to control it now but he still takes everything to heart. He's not flash and wants to play well and do the best for Tottenham.

Ian's dad, Mike, has managed Norwich and Everton so Ian has always been around the game and he's used to it. But I worry. Everything revolves around his career, and it's so short. My dad says if you can't take the heat get out of the kitchen. But sometimes I wish his career was already over or that he was a third-division player so there wasn't so much pressure, and we could just get on with the rest of our lives. I'm a nervous wreck when he's actually playing. I want him to do well and I really feel the pressure. I cried when he made his full England début against Italy in the World Cup qualifying match. I was so proud. But although I had total confidence in his ability, I thought, oh dear, this is one of England's toughest games. Then Zola scored that goal and Ian got terrible stick in the press for days afterwards. But it wasn't his fault – the ball was deflected off Sol Campbell. I felt so sorry for him.

The night before a match I leave him alone and we sleep in separate beds so Ian can get a really good night's sleep. David Seaman's wife says they do the same thing. Actually it's got nothing to do with the sexual side of things, although of course I mentioned it once in an interview and the headlines said NO SEX FOR SUZI ON A FRIDAY NIGHT. The reality is that our dogs sleep with us and there's not a lot of room. They take all the covers and then start barking at about 6 a.m. The media don't realise how demoralising all their criticism is. It upsets me. I find it really difficult that they build you up and then the next day they flatten you. But it is Ian's dream to play for England again.

I didn't know what sort of series the *Cutting Edge* programme was, but I'd signed a release form and my manager said, 'Oh, Suzi, that means whatever you've said and done they can use.' I think they should have been more upfront with me and I was really, really worried before it went out. The thing I was most concerned about was that I didn't have a clue how they were going to put the programme together and when it went out it was in three parts with Samantha Holdsworth, Ann Lee and me, Suzi Walker, the rich bitch, going shopping, trying on clothes. I didn't actually buy anything but they asked to film me going out with loads of bags and at the time I just did it. Straight after that they cut to Jason Lee's wife at home cleaning – I wasn't 100 per cent happy with how that came out. They also filmed me going to look at the house which we then bought, but looking back I don't think I should have let them do that. I wanted to be honest and just ended up being very naive. I have also been too gullible in my dealings with the press, but I know now how people twist things. I've learnt a lot in a short time.

When the programme went out it was the day of Ian's mother's funeral. It was a terrible time because we'd thought she was getting better and then suddenly she took a turn for the worse. She was a wonderfully brave woman and even now I don't think we can believe that she's dead. A couple of weeks after she died I discovered that I was expecting a baby. So if we have a girl her middle name is going to be Jacqueline in memory of Ian's mum.

That programme tried to label me the typical foot-baller's wife – the Page 3 girl, the blonde bimbo. But *huh*, I come from Surrey and I now live in Hertfordshire so there's no hint of Essex! Of course football is fashionable at the moment. There's all sorts of celebrity couples and I think it was Sam Holdsworth's manager who said foot-ballers now hang out with pop stars like Oasis. Well, others might, but Ian doesn't. We hang out with Ian's best friend Roy, who's a plumber, and my best friend Lorraine, who I've known for years. We don't live a 'lifestyle' as such. Unless I'm going out I wear a tracksuit and no make-up – I'm not a glammed-up dolly bird. Most nights Ian watches Sky Sports or the Discovery Channel while I go in another room to watch something like *Coronation Street*.

I can't ever imagine Ian moving. We are Tottenham through and through. I do worry about what would hap-pen if he did ever move, though. Could I accept another club? No, I'd be heart-broken if we had to go and live up north, but I would go because I love him. I also have nightmares about going to play abroad – what would we do with the dogs?

Karen Wigley

Karen Wigley is a senior occupational therapist. Husband Steven began his career at Nottingham Forest and played for clubs including Sheffield United, Birmingham and Exeter. He is now the assistant director of Nottingham Forest's Academy of Football.

My Grandad Moon was a scout for Bolton and it was his suggestion, adopted by the Football Association, that referees should raise their arm to indicate an indirect free kick. So football's always been in my family and I've always liked it. Where we come from in Ashton-under-Lyne, you're either a Manchester City or a Manchester United fan. But because I'm a pain I decided Liverpool were my team.

One of my dad's friends was also a Liverpool fan and he used to take me to Anfield – even to midweek European matches. It was the Kevin Keegan era and I joined his fan club but I remember how mortified I was to discover that it was Kevin's brother, who ran the fan club, who wrote to me, and not my hero.

We used to stand on the Kop, which was always cram, jam-packed. I was only about 11 or 12 years old and I wore my scarf and waistcoat with my Liverpool badges sewn on it – no one wore football shirts in those days. Sometimes my mum came as well and we'd get there early to sit on one of the barriers so that when everyone pushed forward, which they did all the time, you didn't get shoved. I remember once putting my knee up to stop myself being pushed and putting it right between the legs of this guy in front of me. He turned round, his face purple with agony and started effing and blinding at me. My dad's friend was a big 16-stone guy but he didn't need to protect me for long as the bloke I kicked had to leave the ground – it transpired he'd just had a vasectomy. . .

But the crowd never scared me – I loved it. No, the

thing that used to frighten me were the police horses on the walk between the car and the ground. For some reason you weren't allowed to walk the full width of the pavement and these bloody great police horses used to fear me to death because they'd squash you in and we'd be shoved around. Of course it wasn't quite the same atmosphere going to watch Steven play for St Christopher's youth club team – we'd have to walk half a mile down to the pitch and everyone would help carry the goalposts and the footballs.

Wigs and I met at grammar school. He was a year above me but he was in a group of friends that I used to go around with. He left school at 16 and took a job in local government. By this time he was a little disillusioned with football and had stopped playing because although he'd been with some very successful boys' clubs and had a few trials – one at Manchester City – nothing had come of it. But he started playing again just for fun with St Christopher's and got picked up by the local non-league side, Curzon Ashton. Rave reviews followed and then more trials, one at Hereford and then another at Nottingham Forest who decided to take him on.

At the time I was doing my A levels and had decided I wanted to be an occupational therapist. I was applying for various courses and virtually the same week Forest offered Steven a contract I was offered a place at the Derby School of Occupational Therapy, so it worked out really well as we both went down to the same part of the country. Whether we'd still be together if we hadn't, I don't know.

I used to go and watch Steven in the Forest reserves and often found myself getting into arguments. Usually I'd disagree with the idiots I was sitting next to – the thing is, I can't keep quiet if I think they're idiots. I was never one to complain if they were calling my husband.

It didn't have to be Steven. That never bothered me – I've listened to a lot of people calling him over the years. But it was just the general idiocy and I could never resist opening my mouth and telling them what I thought of them. I know it's therapy, bawling at your football team but there are limits. I just lose my patience with people. It almost got me into trouble once. I got sick of this guy next to me smoking in my face. So when he dropped his tobacco, I picked it up and sat on it. He was searching for it everywhere and when he saw it sitting on my seat as I got up to leave, he turned round and swung a punch at me.

Given my inability to keep my mouth shut, it was probably just as well that Brian Clough didn't have too much to do with the wives . . . Steven will never say a bad word against Clough and says he learned a huge amount from him. But it never ceased to amaze me the hold the Forest manager used to have over the players. At training sessions he would get the lads to partner up, with one jumping on the other's back and then the whole silly lot of them had to run through the stinging nettles. I used to say to Steven, 'What do you mean, you *had* to?' 'Well, it's just training,' he'd say. I couldn't understand although I suppose cancelling a morning's training to take the team down a coal mine at the height of the miners' strike was an attempt to broaden their outlook. It was like being in the bloody army – you could never say no.

There were also the bizarre trips that the lads would suddenly take off on. I mean, Steven would literally come home and say they were going to the other side of the world the next day. In fact one year he got a tax rebate because he was out of the country for so long. The trips were to play money-spinning exhibition matches and one was to Baghdad at the height of the Iraq-Iran war. They played their match and had only just left for home when a bomb went off outside their hotel. It's worth pointing out that the manager didn't make that trip. Another time I had booked our summer holiday in romantic Newquay. It was the first one we were ever going to have together – only to discover Clough was taking the team to Kuala Lumpur. This was the off season – my time. But it was all to no avail. So I took a mate instead and had a fantastic time.

Because they were away so much there were all sorts of opportunities for playing around with the legions of women who seem to flock around footballers whether they're good looking or not. But I've never felt threatened by groupies – I suppose it's just a matter of trust. There was one infamous incident involving the Forest lads and a brothel in Amsterdam. They were all supposed to keep the visit secret but one player told his wife, swearing that he was not the one involved and the whole thing came out, with everyone accusing each other of actually doing the dirty deed. Steven's story was that they'd been made to go in: of course, they always followed orders . . . He said he'd had a drink and sat on a barstool, petrified one of these girls would talk to him and the worst that happened was that some of the guys had made small talk. I found the whole thing hilarious. Of course I don't know if he got up to anything or not. I doubt it.

Infamy also attached itself to another Nottingham Forest trip abroad but we all have good reason to be upset about that one because it was when a bent referee cheated us of a place in the UEFA Cup Final. We had been drawn away against the Belgian club Anderlecht in the semi-final in 1984 and contrary to Clough's usual practice he decided to pay for the wives to travel to the match in Bruges. Of course we had a separate hotel. It was very posh. I was into Martini in those days. I ordered the drink and then turned my nose up. How common, I thought – they've put a pickled onion in it. I was so incredibly naive. I remember feeling real embarrassment walking through the red-light district – all those women sitting in windows in their undies.

But the shock of all that was nothing compared to the intimidating atmosphere we found when we got to the stadium. Our seats were very low down and the match had only just started when the Belgians in the tier above started throwing things down at us – bricks, bottles, the seating, you name it. It was frightening. But what was happening on the pitch was even worse. The referee was making some really dodgy decisions. I remember a disputed penalty and Paul Hart's goal, which for no apparent reason was disallowed. But it was the moment that Steven was involved in losing the ball and Anderlecht went down the other end and scored that I recall most vividly. I was mortified. Afterwards the lads got on the same coach as us. They were so disappointed and you knew nothing you could say would help them so there was this terrible silence as we drove to the airport. It didn't help that dozens of Belgian fans were banging on the windows. They players felt cheated at the time. They just couldn't fathom why the decisions had gone against them. Now we find out, all these years later, that they were cheated by the referee, who had been bribed. For Steven it was a particularly bitter blow as this proved to be his only chance of a medal.

After that defeat Brian Clough began to dismantle the team and he made it known that Steven was available. Sheffield United came in but we weren't sure, because they were in the second division. However it seemed that Clough didn't want Steven to go to a top-flight club so we decided to speak to the Yorkshire club. Steven had never done a move before. We didn't have an agent or anything like that and transfers were a lot more secretive than they are today. I was working at a Sheffield hospital at the time so I went with Steven to meet the United manager, Ian Porterfield, and the chairman. They persuaded him and I think he signed without getting a signing-on fee. We had a lovely tuna sandwich at Bramall Lane and I think that's what sold the club to Steven – it coloured his vision.

His stay at Sheffield United proved to be the worst time in his career and was the start of the depressing habit that shortly after any manager signed Steven they were sacked. This time it was Ian Porterfield's turn. Soon after his departure Steven got a very bad groin injury and was told by the club consultant that his career was finished. Fortunately I was working in a medical environment and I was able to get a lot of information from consultants and physiotherapists who were colleagues of mine. We devised a regime of exercises and the Sheffield United physio, to his credit, spent hours and hours working with Steven building up his abductor muscles. But he was out of action for a year, during which time his dad died. I'm afraid the new manager, Billy McEwan, was not very supportive. In fact I don't think he had clue about management. I was so frustrated that I scribbled down my concerns in a letter to the *Sheffield Star*. They printed it but I chickened out at the end: it was signed 'a concerned fan'.

As soon as Steven was fit McEwan sold him to Birmingham City. This time we were very happy with the move. We were able to stay living in Nottingham and John Bond, the Birmingham City manager, gave Steven a car as a signing-on fee. Of course he was then sacked. We'd only been there three months. But Gary Pendry took over and this time Steven flourished under the new management. We also celebrated the birth of our first son Jake in circumstances that can only happen in the mad world of football. I went into labour early one Saturday morning when Steven was away with the team. I think they were playing Barnsley in the FA Cup. I put in a call to the team hotel and Gary Pendry gave Steven permission to race down to Nottingham for the birth. He had only just arrived at the hospital when Jake began to appear. But the cries of 'the head's coming' were drowned out by the voice over the labour suite Tannoy: 'Mr Wigley, Mr Pendry is ringing to find out whether you'll be back in time for the game.' Two minutes later he sped off and was joined by a police escort to the stadium. He arrived at Barnsley's ground, Oakwell, just after two o'clock, scored and was allowed to keep the match ball.

Three years later John Gregory signed Steven for Portsmouth. It won't surprise you to know that shortly after we arrived he was sacked. For the first time in Steven's career we were faced with the prospect of moving house. Well, to be honest I thought I was coming to the end of the earth. Portsmouth seemed to be miles away from anywhere. It was nearly in France, wasn't it? I really didn't want to move and the whole time was a nightmare. I hated it – absolutely loathed it. It didn't help that I had a miscarriage on the day before Steven was due back for pre-season training. But I let him go because I'm a brick like that. The recession had set in, which meant we couldn't sell the house in Nottingham but we took out a bridging loan to buy down south, a financially crippling move.

So here I was not knowing a soul in the world and faced with these weird southerners. I mean, you'd walk into a shop and nobody would speak to you. There was a Texas on the corner and because I was buying a new house I'd often pop in for things like curtain rings and loo brushes. Well, you'd stand there waiting to be served and they'd just ignore you or you'd try and get your car out of the drive and nobody would let you out. Of course over the last eight years I've become as ignorant as them. But when our friend Stuart Gray moved to Southampton FC, where he's now reserve team manager, from Aston Villa, he would take great delight is going up to people and saying 'Morning' and they'd look at him as if he had dog-shit on his face.

I can laugh now but just two weeks after moving in surrounded by boxes and without a phone, Steven came in at 2 a.m. – hours after he'd gone out with the lads for a quick drink after training. I shoved 18-month-old Jake at him and ran out of the house to the phone box. 'Mum, come and get me. I can't stand it.' But instead of running away I did what I always do to keep my sanity – I got a job – a senior post in occupational therapy. I love my work but I'd have to labour a couple of years to earn what some players nowadays earn in a week. Now if Steven had just been ten years younger . . .

At Portsmouth we always seemed to be fighting relegation under Frank Burrows so very soon it was out with him and in with Jim Smith. Steven got on well with him but he was not Smith's kind of player so it was back to reserve team football before being released. Ross, our second son, had been born by then – the birth helped along by a footballing friend letting off fireworks outside my window at 3 a.m. We were fortunate in that Steven found another club when Alan Ball took him down to Exeter. It meant he was now away a lot, which was quite traumatic as I was pregnant again and still working.

I tried to carry on as normal, so one evening, despite the fact that I was nearly nine months pregnant, I went out with Stuart and his wife Kath to watch *Buddy*. It was a super show and I was jiving in the aisles with Kath. However, when I got home I discovered all that dancing had started off my labour. Stuart tried to alleviate the pain by putting a Tens machine on my back but all he ended up doing was nearly electrocuting me.

We decided to leave him with the children and Kath drove me to hospital, with us arguing all the way about the best route. It didn't matter which way we went because we were never going to make it. We were at some traffic lights when I realised Alix had come out. I don't know how long she'd been there but it didn't occur to me to take my trousers off. I think Kath was in shock and she had to open the window because she was so shaky. The poor baby was getting cold but I wouldn't wrap her little body in the shawl we had brought in case it got dirty so I made Kath give me her Armani jacket.

The papers loved the story. The actor who played Buddy came to see us and presented Alix with a plastic plectrum. They wanted me to call her Peggy Sue. But the general footballing feeling was not so upbeat, as the suitability of an ex-Pompey player consorting with Saints' personnel, i.e. Stuart, was mulled over the pints.

Alan Ball was replaced at Exeter by Terry Cooper, and with that Steven's sojourn in league football came to an end. He slipped into non-league football with Bognor Regis. I started working extra days to make up the lost income and we began running a soccer school. It was a difficult transition and it was only part-time, so Steven got a job repping for a bike company. A successful application for the manager's job at Aldershot rescued Steven and at last he found his niche.

Aldershot had once been a league team and they had great ambitions but they were also a friendly little club and Steven flourished. He was out most nights watching matches but he would be around to pick the kids up from school and if they were ill he could take them to Aldershot where his secretary Rosemary would help him take care of them. But of course promotion was the aim, and when after two seasons they just missed out the fans and the papers turned on him. It was the only time our relationship has ever really been affected by football. We argued a lot and Steven was tense and stressed out. So when he was approached by Nottingham Forest to help out with the youth development it wasn't a difficult decision.

Steven moved up to Nottingham in the summer of 1997. I was supposed to follow. But the children didn't want to leave their friends. By now I loved living by the sea and I just couldn't face starting all over again and as Steven knows I'm a bloody horrible person to live with when I'm unhappy. So we're in limbo and the situation has left the family a little unstable, as we now only see Steven on Sundays. But I would never ask him to jack his job in. We'll survive because of something I've always known – he loves me to death.

Suzy Barnes

Suzy is married to John Barnes, one of the most successful footballers of the last decade. He began his career at Watford before moving to Liverpool and Newcastle United and won 79 caps for England.

I used to live with my mum in the house next door to John while he was at Watford. The husband of the lady next door was ill so she had to take in lodgers to earn some money and John, who was 18, lived in the house with Steve Terry, another Watford player. I was with a friend one day and we bumped into John. 'Hello,' he said. 'I'm your neighbour.' When he'd gone my friend said, 'That's John Barnes, the footballer.' The next day I said to someone, 'We've got John Bond living next door to us.'

When I left school I got a steady job in insurance but in a fit of recklessness I gave it up to do something a bit more interesting and went to work on the make-up counter at Miss Selfridge. I loved it – trying make-up on all day, who wouldn't? All the girls used to go out together and we had a good laugh. But I wonder if it was a coincidence that shortly after I first met John he turned up at the counter asking for a bright red lipstick. Oh yes, I thought. What's he here for? Apparently he was going to a fancy-dress party and needed the lipstick for that . . .

After that I used to see John coming and going and then one day he mentioned they only had a black and white television and there was something in particular he wanted to watch so I invited him round and then it became a bit of a habit. I'd come home from work and sit down to my tea and there he'd be, watching television. Obviously I couldn't have fancied him then, otherwise I wouldn't have been able to eat. Gradually he began to pick things off my plate. 'Look,' I'd say. 'If you want something, my mum would be quite happy to make it.' 'No, no,' he'd say, as he pinched another chip.

My friend Tanya lived in the house on the other side of John. We'd grown up together and every Christmas her mum had a party. But this particular year I realised that I was quite keen on John and didn't want to leave him so I said I couldn't go. Unknown to me he was in exactly the same situation. So there we were both pretending we didn't want to go to this do until he confessed and then we went and had a good time. After the party he walked me home – it was only two doors away but we took a detour around the block – and we kissed down the alleyway between our houses.

Funnily enough John's live-in team-mate Steve started dating Tanya and they got married. Sadly they divorced after several years but then Tanya met and married another footballer, Vinnie Jones, now the player-coach at QPR. We do laugh about it as neither of us has any interest in football at all.

Meanwhile John was very happy at Watford. Graham Taylor was the manager at the time and he had a big influence on John's career. He watched him develop and nurtured him. Elton John was our chairman, of course. We would see him occasionally at Watford's ground, Vicarage Road, and I remember a party at his fabulous house. Our first little boy Jamie was only two or three months old and I couldn't bear to be apart from him so I took him with us and it was like a children's playground. Elton and his wife Renata had got in all these Sinclair C5 cars for the lads to race around the garden, that's if they didn't want to play five-a-side football. There was a lady magician to entertain us and running races for the women – I had a go but didn't win – and, I vividly remember, all these gorgeous young waiters. . . I went into the house to use the toilet and noticed an amazing corridor that was lined from ceiling to floor with platinum and gold discs. Then I had a quick look in some of the rooms. One had a huge box full of hundreds of pairs of glasses and another had mirrors on the ceiling and was full of memorabilia from the movie *Tommy*, including this huge pair of boots.

It was while John was at Watford that he scored *that* goal for England against Brazil in Rio. It was a friendly match in the Maracana stadium in the summer of 1984. John picked up the ball on the left wing and just seemed to dance his way through the Brazilian defence. Brian Moore, ITV's football commentator, described it as 'one of the best goals you can ever imagine'. In a lot of ways though it has been a hang-up. John had set himself this incredible standard and then was always having to live up to it. He did, of course. After all, he got 79 caps for England but when towards the end of his international career he got booed at Wembley I just couldn't understand it. It was very upsetting.

But I've got some great memories from John's time with England, particularly from Italia 90 when the FA took all the wives out to Sardinia for a week's holiday. We really were treated like royalty. I remember a shopping trip into Cagliari when we had a huge police escort – six motorbikes at the front and the back of the coach and we were each given an interpreter. The lads would join us on the beach in the afternoons and 3 p.m. was pina colada time when we would send goalkeeper Chris Woods up to the bar for the drinks. I also remember how funny Paul Gascoigne was. Of course it was before Gazzamania and although none of us knew it, probably the last time he could ever be totally relaxed and himself.

Jamie was about three and I was pregnant again when Watford sold John to Liverpool. He went up to Merseyside while I stayed in Watford and tried to decide what to do. It was a mistake because we became a little detached and when I did move up, John had made his own circle of friends. By this time my mother had gone to live in America so I had absolutely no one. It was a very difficult time. Anyone who has just had a baby will know how I felt. I felt very isolated and the last thing I wanted to do was go through all the hassle of trying to make new friends. In fact I was very nervous. Liverpool was a big club. The players were all very well known. You wonder, will they even want to speak to me? So I stayed at home and made no effort to get to know anybody. I just didn't have the confidence. I thought, oh it won't be long and we'll be home again soon. So I decided to move back down south to familiarity and all my old friends. I bought a house in Hemel Hempstead, thinking John will be back soon. Then he phoned to say he'd signed for another year. Oh no – but by then I'd bought the house and I thought, only another year – I'll wait.

We actually spent two years apart commuting up and down the motorway but in a way it was good as it gave me some space and the chance to develop my own personality. For the first time ever I was on my own, no mum to lean on, no John. Footballers are high maintenance and it's very easy to stay in the background, making preparations, waiting for them to come back home – it can be soul destroying. Then I turned it around and decided not to spend the time waiting but to see it as my own time. And then I thought, well what am I going to do with this time? I developed my own life and John had to fit in with me. Instead of me always being available on the off-chance that he had some time to spare, now he had to make the effort to come to me. I became so much stronger, more independent.

It gradually dawned on me that John was becoming a key player at Liverpool, which I'd never expected. It was clear he wasn't going to be coming home. Liverpool was his new home. But by that time I felt more confident and decided to move back up there with him. Up to this point we'd just breezed along but now we wanted to make a big commitment, and decided to get married. Our wedding was the most fabulous day. My mum came over from the States and gave me away. It was in Hemel Hempstead and we tried to keep it a secret but still about 2,000 people turned up and lined the streets. The police had to put barricades up. Imagine if it had been in Liverpool. The press photographers were very good. We gave them five minutes and then said we're off to do our own photos and they left us alone.

When you are in the public eye you have to take the good with the bad. When John and I were living in different parts of the country things were written in the press. The first time you read an article which implies you are not getting on, well, you are devastated. But when it happens again you can't be so upset. Then every so often someone will ask something like, oh we've heard you're selling your house – it's like Chinese whispers – they make it up to suit themselves.

But with the fans it's different. Fans spend a lot of their wages on going to see John. At a pop concert you may get 70,000-odd people but at Liverpool sometimes 40,000 fans turn up twice a week – and only just a few less at Newcastle – so in a way they do own a piece of John, they have invested so much in him. They have every right to ask for his autograph. He is a big part of their lives, he owes it to them to spend a bit of time with them – they don't know they are maybe the fifth or sixth person to speak to him that day. So however busy we are and even if we've got all the children with us, John makes time for everyone.

The fact that John is black was never a problem in my family. The fact that I'm white and he's black was simply never an issue. John's father was a colonel in the

Jamaican army and then he became a diplomat. The family came to England in 1976 and for a time John lived in the Jamaican Embassy. But when I first knew him he wasn't a catch. In fact he wasn't earning a tremendous amount of money in the early days.

When John moved to Liverpool he was one of the first black footballers to play for the team and at first he took a lot of racist abuse which was very upsetting for him. I felt terribly hurt myself. John then began to get involved with the black community, working for example with disadvantaged children in Toxteth, and he gained a lot of respect. Feelings began to change and I think John has been instrumental in helping to break down some of the barriers. I'm not saying that he has single-handedly defeated the problem but a lot of people began to put their racism behind them and started to see John as a person, not just a black face. I am very keyed into the slightest remark which may be racist. Before, I may have let things go, not really having noticed until John pointed out to me the subtler forms of racism which are actually often worse. Now I can spot it a mile off. People often say things carelessly, but they hurt.

Of course I can never forget Hillsborough. We were sat in the main stand very near the Leppings Lane terraces and we could see what was going on. I can remember thinking, oh crikey, why doesn't someone get Kenny Dalglish on the Tannoy and get him to ask everyone to move back. I heard someone saying six people had been killed, then it was 20, then 25. No, this is ridiculous, I thought. It can't be. It was like watching a film. It can't be real. Why were they covering up one guy's face with a jacket? Maybe because he didn't want to be photographed? But how can he breathe? Someone said it's because he's dead. Don't be daft. But then a young boy in front of us having heart massage began to turn blue and it suddenly dawned on us – all those people being taken away on advertising hoardings were dead. All those dead people in front of our eyes and we couldn't do anything but watch. I will never get over it.

John went to as many funerals as he could – sometimes up to three a day. It was so distressing. Liverpool opened Anfield so the relatives could come down and be together. Tea and coffee were laid on and I went in for the first three mornings, talking to the families, going over what had happened. Then after those three days I had a horrendous asthma attack. I couldn't breathe and the doctor had to put me on steroids. I was really stressed for a long time.

We keep in contact with the Hillsborough families and see them each year. People don't realise the suffering that goes on. Last year we met up with a woman whose brother had been killed. She is a complete nervous wreck and hasn't been able to work since. I videoed Jimmy McGovern's docu-drama on the disaster but I haven't been able to watch it yet.

It was an enormous shock to leave Liverpool but I'd suspected it before John did. He'd been dropped for a couple of games but he said it didn't mean anything, they were just trying out some new players. Then they had a match where they put someone else on in the number 10 shirt – John's shirt. He shrugged it off again: 'They're just picking any shirt – it's a friendly.' But I had a niggling suspicion that something was not quite right. I went on holiday and John went in to speak to the manager, Roy Evans, and told him he didn't want to sit on the bench and fade into obscurity so they agreed John should look for a new club. It was a surreal moment when he told me. I remember the phone ringing constantly and John pacing up and down. So I grabbed baby Jasmin, put her in the pushchair and walked out. It was raining but I just walked and walked and walked. I didn't realise they were worrying about me. All I could think about was what's going to happen now? We'd been at Liverpool for ten years. We were adopted Scousers. The people of Liverpool had taken us in and *You'll Never Walk Alone* was our song. All of a sudden we were being plucked away from this. What are we going to do? Where are we going to go? Everything seemed to stop, to stand still, and I couldn't seem to hear anything.

But once John had decided to join Newcastle and link up once again with Kenny Dalglish there wasn't time to think – finding a new house and new schools for the children just took over. And since John has been playing in the black and white he looks younger and fitter and slimmer – it's probably the stripes. His first season at Newcastle was quite incredible. They only just avoided relegation but got through to the FA Cup Final. They were always the underdogs, as Arsenal were going for the double after winning the Premiership but it was a great day out.

Jamie had been to Wembley before but I had promised Jordan that if daddy ever got to a Cup Final again then I would take him. They were both so excited. We flew down to London on the Friday and I took the boys to Planet Hollywood. The hotel where we were staying was full of Geordies and they were singing along to the pianist in the bar. 'Do you know any Oasis?' they asked her. She didn't. 'What about Frank Sinatra, then?' Throughout the weekend all the Newcastle fans every- where had a great time. It was quite amazing in the stadium. 'Stand up if you love the Toon' they sang, so of course everybody did. Arsenal may have won the Cup but the Toon Army definitely outsang them.

We had a meal on the Saturday lunchtime before the game and the guest speaker was Ron Atkinson who has been the manager at clubs such as Manchester United, Aston Villa and Sheffield Wednesday. But to be honest the wives would have preferred the pop band Boyzone as all the football jokes went over many of our heads. In fact some of the wives were so sick with nerves that they couldn't eat. They were so excited, praying that their husbands would do well. But I was much more laid back. I thought that considering Newcastle had almost been relegated it was enough that we had made it to Wembley. John was a substitute and came on with about ten minutes to go in the match when Arsenal were leading 2–0. Every footballer thinks he can change the game but it was not to be, and he was very disappointed. I was also aware more than I have ever been of how devastated the players on the losing team feel. But Jamie and Jordan had a good day out and were very taken with their daddy's runners-up medal.

Of course both Jamie and Jordan would like to emulate their dad and play at Wembley but John tells them never to pin their hopes on being a footballer. He tells them to study like mad and then if you're lucky enough to get spotted, well, it's a lovely life – you do something you enjoy and you get paid for it. John has always been good with the boys but it was only after our first little girl Jemma was born that I realised what a besotted dad he'd become. She is his little ballerina, although at the moment she wants to be a policewoman.

In the early years when John's football took him away a lot, when the phone was constantly ringing or I couldn't open the papers without reading about him, I did feel harassed by the life of a football wife. Now I am much more relaxed and John has matured a lot. When you are young it is very flattering to have all this attention but of course it is only because you are a footballer. John's fan mail used to be young girls writing to say they adored him and were blonde and blue-eyed, and they just happened to include their phone numbers. Nowadays, because John does a lot of TV commentary as well, when he always looks very smart in a suit, he has become the housewives' favourite. We've gone from the glam girls giggling and eyeing him up to the housewives admiring him as a family man. That suits me just fine.